Innocent Aboard

CHAY & MAUREEN BLYTH

Innocent Aboard

Adlard Coles
Erroll Bruce
Richard Creagh-Osborne

Nautical House
Lymington, Hampshire

**Nautical
Publishing
Company**

in association with George G. Harrap & Co. Ltd.,
London, Toronto, Sydney, Wellington

SBN 245 50480 X

First published in 1970 by
NAUTICAL PUBLISHING COMPANY
Nautical House Lymington Hampshire

Printed in Great Britain by
Compton Press Compton Chamberlayne Salisbury

For Samantha Fiona
who unknowingly had to wait

Acknowledgements

When you can't sail or navigate and you plan to go around the world non-stop, you have to turn to friends and experts for quite a bit of advice and assistance. In my case hundreds of people were involved, and to all of these I am indeed grateful and indebted. I would like to say a special 'thank you' particularly to these kind people : –

R. A. G. Nierop of Westfield Engineering who took a chance by lending me *Dytiscus,* and without whose assistance I would have been a spectator. Neville Wood of Windward Sailing School for his encouragement and patience while teaching me the basics of navigation and sailing. Frank and Audrey Allen – for their encouragement and assistance and also for lending me their sextant. John Slim of *The Birmingham Post* for all his work, help and co-operation in the writing of this book. Chris Waddington of Wicomarine, without whose assistance, and the facilities of his yard, I would not have been ready in time. Mammy, who looked after Samantha and made our return trip together possible. Charlie Brooker for ensuring that my mast was in order. Bill Cottell for the loan of his jury rig and extra water containers. Jack Gregory for loaning me his compass and supplying me with endless numbers of socks. John Deacon for his assistance in making the radio available. Capt Neil McAllister of *Gillian Gaggins* for petrol so that I could aagin charge my batteries. Charlie Gough for his endless efforts to get my needs in South Africa. Bill and Betty Ridley, Brian Cooke, members of the Royal Southern Yacht Club, Dave Gibbins, Lt Cdr W. J. Meyers, David Russell, R. Hughes, Tony and Margaret Marshall, my sister Isobel, Michael Bearn, Dr H. Wilkinson, E. Downey, E. Robinson, Trevor Juniper, Paul Sargent.

I would like to thank these companies which were generous in helping the venture : –

The Dunlop Co., Ltd., for their Dirti-Weather suit and liferaft. Schermully Ltd. for their flares. Smiths Industries for chronometer. Jeckells Ltd. for their sails. Batchelors Foods Ltd. Gillette. Lucas for their batteries. Norseman Terminals for their rigging. S.P. Radio. Nikonos for their underwater camera. South Western Marine Factors. Dewars Ltd. for their whisky, and South Coast Dairies for other refreshment. Also Honda Ltd. for their help.

As this book goes to press we heard with deep regret of the sudden death of Bill Ridley who gave such great encouragement to the enterprise.

Contents

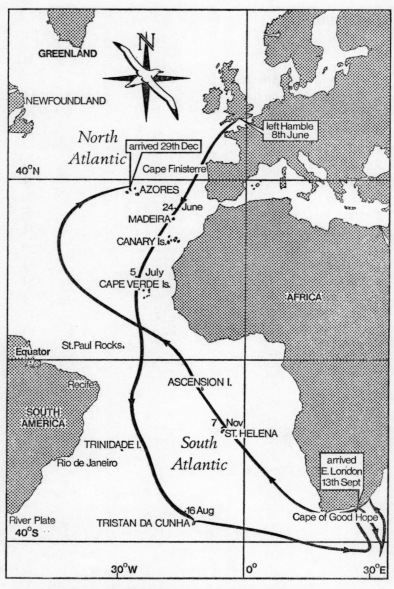

N

GREENLAND

NEWFOUNDLAND

North Atlantic

40°N

left Hamble 8th June

arrived 29th Dec

Cape Finisterre

AZORES

24 June

MADEIRA

CANARY Is.

5 July
CAPE VERDE Is.

AFRICA

St.Paul Rocks.

Equator

Recife

ASCENSION I.

SOUTH AMERICA

7 Nov
ST. HELENA

TRINIDADE I.

Rio de Janeiro

South Atlantic

arrived E. London 13th Sept

16 Aug

TRISTAN DA CUNHA

Cape of Good Hope

River Plate

40°S

30°W   0°   30°E

Track of *Dytiscus III* to the Roaring Forties and back

Foreword by Sir Alec Rose

Chay Blyth, after only a few hours of instruction under sail, and sailing a handful of miles in sole charge of his boat, set out from the Hamble River in a small family cruiser, beat his way out of the English Channel, found his sea legs crossing the Bay of Biscay, worked past Madeira and into the Trade winds, weathered the bulge of South America, and then carried right on down the South Atlantic to test his skill even in the Roaring Forties before he decided that it was asking too much of his shallow-draught bilge-keel boat to aim for Cape Horn.

It was a disappointment to Chay that he had to abandon his first attempt to sail alone round the world, but I feel certain that he made a seaman's decision in this. His boat was a splendid little craft for her designed task; but this was not running for thousands of miles before the huge seas of the Roaring Forties.

Thus he put into harbour and cabled to his wife, Maureen, to join him for the long sail back home. She came at once, and her first experience of a sailing boat was to set out with Chay into the Southern Ocean which, off South Africa, is often stirred into a maelstrom as the Aghullas Current fights against the westerly gales.

For both of them it was a remarkable achievement, but I hope that no one will be misled by their delightfully light-hearted story, often told in land language instead of sea terms, into thinking that their venture was casual.

Chay certainly had very little sailing experience when he set out in command of his sailing boat, but he had gained great knowledge of the sea in really small craft by rowing across the Atlantic with John Ridgway; as a soldier he was very well practised in the art of looking after himself in difficult situations – including the Arctic and tropics. He had also judged well in those he had asked for advice; with their help he planned and prepared for his voyage with meticulous care.

Most of all this voyage was a human feat. Here was a young married couple, in some ways just an ordinary young couple like millions of others; yet he was determined to test himself against difficulties which seemed almost impossible, and she backed him with unfailing loyalty.

It gives me great faith in the future that we have such young men as Chay Blyth and Robin Knox-Johnston. And also that we have such young women as Maureen Blyth.

I

The Birth of a Notion

Chay Blyth

I wish the nation's trouser-makers had never invented pockets. Admittedly, the thought had never occurred to me in the quarter of a century or so that I had been a delighted user of their products – right up to 1042 hours on June 8, 1968. But then, with the uncomfortable feeling that the world was watching, the utter regrettability of the pockets with which I was provided came upon me in a blinding flash of consternation.

If I turned a fetching shade of sheerest sunrise, I can only hope that the world was not watching too closely after all – and that the subsequent burst of faked but frantic activity in which I indulged was sufficient to hide my confusion.

The scene that bright June morning was the Hamble, the river-mouth home of the Royal Southern Yacht Club just off Southampton Water. A flotilla of assorted craft was grouped purposefully on the sparkling millpond surface. Upstart dinghies bobbed cockily in the lee of majestic sea-going yachts, which remained patently un-impressed by such presumption. Motorboats snarled bad-temperedly among the sails which sought to harvest the force four breeze.

Billowing blues and reds and whiter-than-whites tacked and counter-tacked, with collision constantly on the cards. Television launches manoeuvred determinedly with a view to a view, their cameramen marvellously unmoved by the proceedings as they gave their undivided attention to their lenses.

It was all, I could not help feeling, a bit more exciting than I would have wished, given the chance to state my preferences. My problem was that I was a novice sailor where a novice sailor has no right to be : on the deck, and in sole charge, of a 30ft bermudan-rigged sloop, slap in the middle of all that multi-coloured activity and heading uncompromisingly out to sea.

When I say I was a novice sailor, I mean just that – and then

11

some. As a solo navigator, the only experience I could point to was
eight hours of making myself an unexpected menace to other boats
as I fumbled my way round Langstone Harbour, plus one unimpres-
sive venture out to sea which had failed to take me out of sight of
land before I became becalmed near the Nab Tower, three miles
off Portsmouth.

On June 8, therefore, with just six miles under my belt, I was
in no danger of being mistaken for Christopher Columbus. Close
friends, with only my welfare at heart, had pointed me the way I
wanted to go, set my sails and my self-teering gear, and left me to
my own highly uncertain devices aboard the good ship *Dytiscus III*.

On reflection, they were probably too kind. They had left me
with absolutely nothing to do. But at the time, apart from the
butterflies and the reservations inseparable from the pageantry of the
occasion, I was utterly grateful to them.

I stood in the sunshine, listening to the slap of the sails and the
chuckle of the bow wave, and offered up a silent thank-you – both
to the characters who had done the actual physical bit of setting me
on my way a few moments earlier, and to a whole list of people
who had rallied round in the hectic months of which this was the
climax. Neville Wood, Frank Allen, Bill Cottell, Bill Ridley, Brian
Cooke, Charlie Brooker – they were just half a dozen of something
like fifty people who had done all they could help me try to prise
the practicable out of the impossible.

And, above all, there was my wife. Maureen. The girl with me
and baby Samantha in the photograph that I had propped up in the
galley. What a girl! As tension had mounted in the final weeks of
preparation, I had been something of a handful. She had had more
to put up with than I could reasonably have expected of her, but
she had met my irritability with nothing but loyalty. She had stayed
up late at night planning menus, working out an index showing
where every piece of equipment was stored, packed food and
'surprise' parcels in heat-sealed polythene bags. She had travelled
miles in search of scores of separate items that I was going to need
in the future which was now almost upon me. She . . . .

Bang!

The sudden report from the starting gun brought me back to
earth. Or rather, it reminded me I was on my way to sea and doing
nothing whatever to help myself get there any quicker. Startled, I
became aware again of my surroundings; took in the number of

Press photographers on the boats; gulped unhappily as I foresaw a million readers' reactions to tomorrow morning's newspaper pictures.

"Good God – he's going round the world with his hands in his pockets!"

It was time to try to look as if I meant business. I began walking about. I leaned over things, examining them with exaggerated intensity. I tugged importantly at shackles. I did not know what the devil I was supposed to be doing – but I hoped I was creating the right impression.

My aim, that summer's day, was to go round the world non-stop. Admittedly, I would have given more for my chances if I had happened to have any practical experience of navigation to add to my six miles of solo seamanship, and if my boat had been something more than a bilge-keeled shallow-draft craft designed purely for family cruising.

But at least it was going to make a change from rowing the North Atlantic and falling out of aeroplanes.

* * * * * *

My departure in *Dytiscus III* came just two years and four days after John Ridgway and I had stepped into the 20ft dory, *English Rose III,* at Cape Cod, Massachusetts. We were two paratroopers who unwittingly caught the world on the hop by announcing our intention of rowing to Britain – a goal which we achieved when we came ashore three months later.

John and I got to know each other pretty well in the ninety-two days which we spent at the mercy of the sea in the summer of 1966. You don't pass three months as a tobogganning two-some on murderous green mountains without establishing a formidable rapport. We came through the same hell together, pushed by the same driving force – an interest amounting to a compulsive curiosity in discovering what the human frame can tolerate. Survival, you may say, is our subject. It was no surprise to me when I discovered in January 1968 that John was set on survival again, this time the solo circumnavigational way in a thirty-foot yacht which he had christened *English Rose IV.* I must say I envied him that name. I had hoped to call the boat I borrowed *The Spirit of English Rose* – not out of a sturdy Scottish sense of commercialism as much as sentiment – but that was an ambition which didn't come off.

English Rose IV set off on June 1, seven days before my trouser pockets were to become the most prominent feature of the Hamble. John's starting point was the Aran Isles, which was where *English Rose III* had brought us home on an unforgettable September evening. Sentiment or commercialism? I must ask him some time! John's boat, like *Dytiscus III,* was a thirty-foot bilge-keeled job in glass fibre. Survival two years earlier had been a team affair : this time, it had just got to be considered as a race. It would have been considered as a race in any case, of course, thanks to the enter-prise of *The Sunday Times,* although both of us had in fact been well advanced in our preparations before there was any question of a newspaper's sponsoring a round-the-world adventure, and although I never even got as far as completing an entry form.

As far as I was concerned, it was Sir Francis Chichester and *Gipsy Moth IV* who first started me considering the possibilities of my going global – and even then it happened in two stages. He arrived home on May 28, 1967, when I was still a sergeant in the Parachute Regiment and not due for release from the Army until the following November.

At that time, I was making my contribution to the peace effort by travelling the country giving lectures aimed at stimulating interest in the Army. Wherever I went, I found I was meeting yachtsmen or characters who were interested in adventure. I suppose four men out of five start life with a natural attraction to adventure, but commonsense prevails as succeeding years surround them with a rampart of responsibilities to their firm and their family, and they throw in their hopes and reach for a bowler hat. It's entirely under-standable : it's chaps like me who are the odd-balls. But then, bowler hats have never really suited me : I think I would rather have people pointing at my trouser pockets than heralding my headgear.

But even though most people see the light before they become involved in half-witted exercises like the ones which I find irresist-ible, they still have imaginations which are readily kindled and enthusiasms which respond to the stories of somebody else's adven-tures. And when Sir Francis had been safely restored to us, his achievement was the talking point which always rounded off my lecture sessions. The comments would range from the cynical but envious *He must be bonkers* to the open and ungrudging approval which was couched in such adjectives as *Terrific!* and *Incredible!* But always the high spot of the discussion would come when somebody chipped in with : *I suppose all that's left now is to go round the world non-stop.*

In the circles in which I was moving, the gospel of going non-stop was following me like a tail light. If I had begun taking bets about the probability of its being preached, I could have made myself a small fortune. The odd thing was, it never struck me that the hypothetical windswept whizz-kid about whom we were constantly speculating might possibly be me. As far as I was concerned, it would be some other fellow—a man with years of yachtsmanship behind him, an unquestioned expert in the ways of the sea. In my own mind, I simply never got to the starting line.

This is not to say that Sir Francis did not make any impact on me. On the contrary, I was jumping up and down as enthusiastically as everybody else – and because I am the itchy-footed individual that I am, I was intent on doing something about it. I knew, that is to say, that like the man in the poem I must go down to the sea again; that there would be no peace for my friends and family until I had satisfied my newly found compulsion to find fulfilment under sail.

But my sights – oddly, in retrospect – were set on the 1968 solo transatlantic race : all the talk of a single-handed circumnavigation somehow failed to fire me to the logical reaction – namely, that I should try to go one better than Sir Francis and go round the world without stopping. I did not really pause to take an objective look at my line of reasoning. By my cag-handed calculations it seemed that the Atlantic was the obvious starting point for my new sailing aspirations. I had rowed the Atlantic without having been able to row before I stepped into *English Rose:* what more logical than that I should consider the same tumultuous ocean the rightful place for Chay Blyth, non-sailor, to have his first sail?

But I failed completely to contemplate going round the world. Moderation in all things : that would have been ridiculous!

The idea that sailing had something to offer me came in the spring of 1967, when Sir Francis was battling his way through the Roaring Forties towards Cape Horn and everybody at home was anxiously watching his progress. At this time, of course, my solo sailing experience did not even amount to those pitiful six sea miles which I tried to keep quiet about in the weeks immediately preceding my departure in *Dytiscus III.* By the spring of 1967, I had sailed not a solitary nautical inch – but I wanted to sail the Atlantic.

My hope, plus my interest in learning how to handle a boat, appeared in one of the newspapers which serve the Portsmouth area where I live. Readers who married the scope of my ambition to the extent of my experience could have been forgiven for wondering which institution I had escaped from.

If Neville Wood had similar thoughts, he kept them to himself. There was no hint in the letter which he wrote to me on April 18 that what he had read in the Portsmouth *Evening News* had caused him to boggle either at my mental processes or at my sublime cheek. He is the proprietor of the Windward Sailing School, which he runs from Langstone Harbour, and a member of the Eastney Cruising Association, who had made me an honorary member the previous month. I was tickled, incidentally, by the letter which Mrs E. W. Jackson, the association's membership secretary, had sent me with my member's certificate. She wrote: 'Dear Sgt. Blyth, I am happy and most honoured to welcome you as a member of the E.C.A. Enclosed are your membership card, book of rules and safety litera-ture, the last of which does not seem to mention safety harness for Atlantic crossings!

'We found your book, *A Fighting Chance,* much more exciting than any whodunnit. What a wonderful gift is such unruffable good humour as yours. As far as was possible from our armchairs, we lived each day of the journey with you until you were safely home.

'Everyone at the club hopes to see you as often as your time allows and we send you and Mrs Blyth our best wishes at all times.'

Then came Neville's letter: if I were not already fixed up, he would be pleased to teach me how to sail. He presumed I wanted to learn cruising, in which case the yacht concerned would be the one on the front of his brochure. 'There would be no charge as you are a member of E.C.A. and in admiration of your Atlantic crossing . . . .''

Coming out of the blue as it did, this was quite incredible. I had never met Neville Wood, and here he was offering me the benefit of his vast experience and his professional services, just like that. But I must say I paled a trifle when I looked again at that yacht on the brochure: it was heeling dauntingly to starboard at the head of a white-waved wake, and whatever was going on at the time the camera shutter clicked looked frantically exciting from my viewpoint as a nautical innocent.

A bit irreligiously, and not for the first time, the thought crossed

my mind that it is quite remarkable how yachtsmen spend considerable sums of money on buying themselves the latest in sailing boats
and in fitting it with the latest in sailing equipment – and how,
once they are under way, all that happens is that they give their
feet a ride while they sit in the water. Utter heresy, of course : my
only defence is that I had everything to learn – including the
difference between cruising and dinghy sailing.

Learning started on Saturday, April 29, 1967. By then, I had
invested in a sailing suit, sailing boots and sailing shoes. I had a
feeling that my presence was going to incline heavily towards the
ornamental – I could not even decide which of my two types of
footwear I ought to favour – but at least I was going to do what I
could to look as if I meant business.

Neville, a former chief petty officer in the Royal Navy, turned
out to be a compact, bouncy figure, fair-haired and friendly; but
there was a natural shyness which made him appear to be a little on
the hesitant side. We shook hands, then we piled into his speedboat
with four of his pupils and buzzed meaningfully over to meet the
boat of the brochure. This was *Tarantana*, a thirty-six-foot sloop
with white hull, grey superstructure and white sails. I could not help
feeling just a little reassured by the calm majesty with which it was
sitting at its mooring : it looked to be a far more solidly reliable
affair than that action photograph had led me to expect.

We climbed aboard. I decided the best thing I could do was to
keep quiet and watch. Smoothly, speedily, sailing's essential pre-
liminaries were carried out. Wonderingly, I took in my first glimpse
of the mysteries of my strange new world; breathed silent admiration
through both nostrils as Neville and his youthful protégés went
through what was obviously a virtually automatic routine. In no time
at all, we were under way.

It was a beautiful morning. All round us, boats were busying
about the harbour, grateful for the benediction of sun and breeze,
and those craft which were still at their moorings were straining
at their leashes like multi-coloured puppies anxious to join in the
business of the day. This was my first taste of the atmosphere of
boating. Ahead, I could see the eastern tip of the Isle of Wight,
the background to a blue, inviting sea across which scores of sails
were making effortless progress. Effortless? As I say, I had everything
to learn.

Meanwhile, on the boat whose progress was of more immediate

interest to me, Neville and his pupils were settling to their individual duties with purposeful competence. Their conversation, if it could be called that, came in gusting bursts above the swish of the water and the hiss of the breeze through the rigging. And always it was on a level that was strictly practical. Small talk was out; sea talk was in. I listened bemused to an interchange of shouts containing references to halyards, fore-and-afts, sheets and pulpit; then I looked hopefully at the big white screen which was the mainsail, just in case anybody thought of putting up the sub-titles. They might just as well have been spelling it out in Swahili. I could see I had been left firmly at the post.

The odd thing was that Neville's four-lad crew seemed to be under the impression that I knew all about sailing. They did not realise that that Atlantic business the previous year had been my first encounter with the sea. Funny, too, that these youngsters could handle this thirty-six-foot cruising yacht and they had not been further than the Isle of Wight – whereas I had come three thousand five hundred miles through two hurricanes and did not know the first thing about our present exercise.

I stayed uncertainly out of the way and went on watching.

Neville was preoccupied with his pupils, as was only proper. Before accepting his invitation, I had made it clear that I simply wanted to start by looking and listening, and that he was to ignore me. After all, the youngsters were paying for the privilege of learning what seamanship was all about, and I was just a guest.

As I watched, I was forcibly struck by the change in my host. The diffidence, the awkwardness, had disappeared. Aboard *Tarantana,* he was on his home ground and he knew that ground like the back of his weather-beaten hands. He was a seaman at one with his ship. From that moment, my confidence in this compact, unassuming character began to grow. And with each succeeding lesson, it was to grow some more.

But would I ever learn to handle a boat like this one? I could not help feeling that there seemed to be an awful lot of it. Inevitably, I found myself comparing it with the only other boat of which I had first-hand sea-going knowledge. Down below were four bunks, a toilet, sail lockers, and a galley with a cooker that was gimbled to keep it horizontal whatever the angle of the yacht.

Life aboard *English Rose III* had offered nothing like it.

I came to know *Tarantand's* galley pretty well that summer. I never really overcame the sheer embarrassment of my unquestioned superfluity to the proceedings on deck, and I kept away from the tiller like a saint avoiding sin once I had discovered that the way I was supposed to make the boat go and the way the boat in fact went had a habit of being quite remarkably unrelated.

That first trip, I established myself as the coffee man. It was a move which kept me admirably out of trouble, and I pledged myself devotedly to maintaining a ceaseless supply to the fellows upstairs who were doing all the work. All the same, the matter which remained uppermost in my mind was *The Observer* 1968 Single-Handed Transatlantic Race. When my first day's sailing was over, I went back with Neville to his home in Southsea : I wanted to know how long it would take me to be ready to face the Atlantic under sail, and I was hoping Neville would come up with the answer.

While his wife, Wynne, rallied round with the sandwiches and coffee – I was happy to hand over my prerogative once I stepped ashore – which she was to provide so unfailingly and so willingly in the months to come, Neville chewed thoughtfully on my question. When he spoke, it was to ask a question of his own : did I want to enter to win, or would I be content to finish?

I know my limitations, despite assertions to the contrary made by people who have been looking up the record books. I said I had no illusions about beating Eric Taborly.

Neville shrugged.

'In that case, four weeks, full time.'

'*What!*'

I almost shouted the word. I had been expecting to have to face long months of preparation. Disbelief came at full throttle as I said that four weeks did not seem very long, considering the breadth and scope of my present status in seamanship.

He smiled, and produced the explanation.

'If you said you were sailing to the Channel Islands or the French ports, you would need a lot longer. The danger in sailing is not when you are at sea – at least, not if you have a sound boat, which we must assume you will have . . . .'

That was a thought, of course. At the moment, I was quite devastatingly boatless. I was sitting here, sipping Wynne Wood's coffee and knowing roughly as much about navigation and seaman-ship as the family dog did, and blithely hoping that person or persons unknown would be prepared to trust several thousand pounds' worth of yacht to me and the Atlantic breakers. But that was something I had to think about a bit later. I listened some more.

'The danger is near to the coast. That is when you have to know your charts, currents, lee shores and rocks, and all about the buoyage system.

'The solo transatlantic is different. If you can get over the starting line all right, you will be able to handle her by the time you reach New York. What we have to concentrate on are the rudiments.

'And in any case, you won't be able to enter unless you have qualified by doing a five hundred-mile solo trip – and that will teach you all you need to know. There's no quicker way to learn than to be on your own.'

His words brought memories of hundreds of tons of foaming white waves roaring towards me in the hurricanes the previous year. Those were the times when John and I had felt frighteningly on our own; the times when *Rosie* had seemed to come alive, rearing and tossing in the seas in spite of the gallons of water she had shipped.

They were the times when the wind screamed like some hysterical animal and threw forty-foot waves at us in a fury which was nothing short of demonic.

I gave an unintentional little shiver; pulled myself back to the present. Neville was talking about navigation.

'As we are concerned only with the race, we can concentrate on astro. It's not as if you're going to be in charge of a big liner or merchant vessel, where other people's lives are involved and where every day at sea costs your company money.

'It won't take as long as you might think. You mustn't worry. If your sight puts you more than ten miles from land, you will be all right – and if it puts you near land, you can sail away and then sail back again when it's light. You can usually see land between twenty and sixty miles away, depending on visibility and how high the land is, so I shouldn't get too anxious about it.'

When I left Neville's home late that night, my think bubble was full of asterisks and most of them were doing handsprings. I had what is technically known as Food For Thought. What had seemed a sheer impossibility just a day or two ago, at the time my ambition and my incompetence had found their way into the newspaper story, now actually appeared to have a chance of coming to pass.

Next night, in the sergeants' mess at Aldershot, I sat down and began to draw up a detailed plan of how I was going to organise myself to have a yacht and to be fully equipped. And in spite of my diffident reply to Neville, I found I was cherishing an insistent little hope that I might find I was in the market for miracles and that I might either win or at least sail into one of the leading placings. Sometimes I think my surname could not sound more suitable for me if it sat up all night working at it.

There were plenty of problems, even if I discounted my current inability to distinguish between splicing the mainbrace and tacking to port. I was still in the Army, still giving lectures which demanded a lot of travelling and gave little free time. Moreover, demobilization was due in November and I had to find civilian employment before it arrived. And my wife was with her mother in Newcastle, awaiting the arrival of our first baby, so my weekends regularly went on pilgrimages north.

It was obvious I was going to miss most of the good weather, and in any case I had to fit in with Neville's plans because he was earning his living from his school. I was not free to sail very often, and sometimes when I was it happened that he was teaching dinghy sailing, which meant that we could not go cruising.

In all that summer, I had seven day trips with him and his pupils. And every time, the futility of my efforts to make myself useful caused me to retreat to the galley, from where I emerged inter- mittently with the shout which had become my trademark : *Who wants more coffee?*

I was the innocent aboard—and by this time even the pupils knew it.

But innocence was to become transparent idiocy. It happened on Saturday, June 3, 1967. That is a date I am unlikely to forget. It is the date when an untried tyro who had until then modestly limited his ambitions to beating the world's best yachtsmen across the Atlantic suddenly got a personal fix on that other seafaring topic – the topic which he had discussed intermittently but disinterestedly for months.

Maureen and I were driving from Newcastle to my home town, Hawick, in Roxburghshire, to visit one of my five sisters. It was a journey we had done many times. The solo transatlantic was a subject which had become part of our lives, and we thrashed it remorselessly as we followed the familiar sixty-mile route up the A 696 through Belsay and Kirkwhelpington to Otterburn, and then

on to the A 68 to skirt the Catcleugh reservoir before we entered
the home straight which contains names like Carter Bar, Southdean
and Bonchester Bridge.

Familiar route, familiar topic. But then, without giving Maureen
a preliminary hint that I was about to explode in her right ear,
I woke up to the realization that my goal, crazy though it was,
yet was needlessly limited. What prompted my revelation, I still
have no idea. What I do know is that without warning the car was
resounding with the evidence that light had at last dawned.

'Hell!' I shouted. 'Why don't I do what Francis did – but do it
non-stop?'

2

"A Boat, A Boat"

Chay Blyth

*M*Y new target was exactly the spur I needed. It had new problems and they were bigger ones. It had an impressively lunatic impossibility when considered in conjunction with my inability to handle a sea-going yacht. It was a crazy goal and it was one I simply had to go for. Why it took me so long to get round to aiming at it, I still do not know. But when I did get round to it, it was like having a new lease of life. For the rest of that trip to Hawick, and for the whole of the return journey to Newcastle when the weekend was over, Maureen and I mangled the idea of a non-stop circumnavigation.

The thing that had to be settled before I started to square up to the realities of the trip itself was the equal reality of life for the girl I would be leaving behind me. This was a factor which sat squarely on my conscience, and one which I could not possibly resolve on my own. Morally, had I the right to abandon Maureen, whose at present unborn child would probably be less than a year old when I left her? Had I the right to leave her with no guarantee that I would be spared to come back to her? Had I the right to leave her, not only to tackle the unknown quantity of parenthood without me but burdened by the worry of where I was and how I was?

It was only last summer that she had spent three months wondering if a twenty-foot rowing boat was going to keep me safe from everything the North Atlantic could throw at me. Could I possibly commit her to a similar, but longer, trial so soon?

Her answer was decisive and unshakable. It stood four-square against every argument I could muster as to why I ought to behave like a rational human being and stay at home – and believe me, I mustered a whole battery of them : the Blyth conscience has a kick like a well-primed carthorse.

Simply, firmly, quietly, in that attractive Geordie-tinged accent

23

of hers, she said : 'I shall be all right. You will have enough to
worry about without worrying over me.'

And from that she would not budge. Even after the birth of little
Samantha Fiona, the baby daughter who has come to mean everything to us, on July 19, she still would not budge. As I fussed about
my new little family, with proud fatherhood written all over me,
I marvelled again at the strength which lay behind such loyalty.
I myself drew strength from it – but that did not prevent my feeling
that I was setting a new standard in caddishness by taking advantage
of it. From then on, however, the trip was 'on'. In the months to
come, Maureen and I became a stronger team than ever, united in
our determination to take impossibility by the scruff of its neck
again. With a wife who backed me every inch, I just had to have a
crack at going the way that Chichester had gone.

But who was going to provide the boat, or the cash to buy one?
I had no boat of my own : paratroop sergeants do not normally
rise to possessing ocean-going yachts, and I was no exception.

I had to find a firm or a person prepared to back a nautical
know-nothing, and nobody had to kick me in the ankles to make me
appreciate the problem. It was not, however, a problem which held
out no hope of solution : my North Atlantic trip had left me with a
wake of acquaintances in the yachting fraternity. Here, surely, was
my obvious starting point.

Round about this time, however, various distractions like preparing for my demobilization were getting in my way and it was
some time before I managed to write to Bill Ridley. He is an ex-
paratroop sergeant who is now responsible for *The Birmingham Post
and Evening Mail* Boat and Leisure Life Exhibition, which is held
in Birmingham every year. His reply to my letter showed that he
was prepared to help me in my search for a sponsor. Maureen and
I travelled to his home in Solihull, Warwickshire, and there we
drafted the first letter. It was October 17.

I outlined my hopes of seeing the world solo and non-stop, and
I added : 'With the tremendous experience that I gained on my row
across the Atlantic, I am very confident that with the proper planning and preparation this is definitely possible.' Needless to say, I
was not quite as confident as that sounded, but one has to put a bold
face on things sometimes.

Then came three weeks of waiting. They were ended by the
arrival of a letter which was polite and to the point – four sentences

long, with the nub of the thing in the third one: 'It is, however, with much regret that I have to tell you that we have decided that it is not possible to help financially.' The Americans would call it a don't-call-me-I'll-call-you letter.

It was all I could reasonably have expected, but it was a smack in the eye for the hopes I had unreasonably entertained. I incline towards a cocky optimism which is often the despair of my immediate circle, and by the time that letter arrived I had armed myself to the teeth with files full of facts and plans. I had prepared my answers – some of them necessarily circuitous – to the sort of questions I expected to be asked when I was invited to an interview: after all, when you are asking somebody to trust you to take his boat round the world and he asks you what sailing you have done so far, you cannot just say 'None.' It would be the ultimate in conversation-stoppers, a four-letter word without a future.

As I should have foreseen, that first reply, early in November, 1967, set the pattern of the replies which were to follow. I tried boat-builders, engineers, brewers, food and clothing manufacturers. I must have written a hundred-and-fifty letters. Maureen saw that the regular arrival of replies which said the same thing in so many different ways was beginning to get me down. She refused to show me that she thought my chances of finding a boat were pretty slender. Instead, she encouraged me to a renewed bout of letter-writing. And more than that: she said that if we did not find a boat by Christmas we could sell our bungalow and buy one of our own. It was yet another example of the unswerving loyalty which she gave me without question, but this was taking loyalty too far: I could not seriously contemplate tiping her out of her home as a sort of bonus to my proposed abandonment of her for 12 months – even when Christmas produced a letter from the Hawick Knitwear Manufacturers' Association which left me realizing that if local boy was going to make good he would have to make it without the locals.

I could not blame the knitwear men any more than I could blame the brewers and the boat-builders. How could I expect anyone attuned to the commonsense of commerce to link himself with the incipient idiocy which I was thrusting under his startled nose?

One firm got as far as offering me six thousand pounds, which we estimated would be half my expenses. Heady at finding someone with the faith I had almost ceased to hope for, I emerged from the interview and whooped the good news to Maureen. We were like two children at our first party : things were moving at last. Now nothing was going to stop me finding the other half. A Southampton boatbuilding firm heard me out with interest ; a designer prepared preliminary sketches showing modifications which the experts thought would be necessary. I showed them to Neville Wood, who agreed that they seemed reasonable. My sponsor said he would write to the boat-builders, assuring them of his confidence in me. The jigsaw puzzle was falling into place.

Two weeks later, I had another letter from my sponsor. I stared at it, shattered : he had decided to withdraw.

Somehow, there always seems to be a bright side. John Deacon, head of a Southampton firm of civil engineers, whom I had never met before, arrived at my home in his Rolls Royce one night in January, 1968, to take me to address the Southampton Lions – and he took me completely aback by offering to buy and pay for the installation of a radio telephone. This was a five-hundred-pound luxury which I had resolved to do without, because every pound I spent meant a pound less for Maureen when I had gone – assuming, that is to say, that I ever found a boat in which to go. He was insistent, despite my protests that I could not possibly accept such a gesture, unrelated as it was to any question of a return in advertising benefits.

There were many times that summer, after receiving a cable from Maureen, that I thanked God for the result of that night drive to Southampton.

As far as finding a boat was concerned, the managing director of the boatbuilders said that I was not to give up just yet. He would look into the chances of his firm providing the yacht. I teetered on the uncertain tightrope between triumph and despair. At the end of January, the uncertainty was ended : the boat-builders could not help, either.

There was still another string to the Blyth bow, however. Before Christmas, Brian Cooke, a Poole bank official who was going to justify his entry in the 1968 solo transatlantic race by coming fifth, had put me in touch with the Westfield Engineering Company (Marine) Ltd, of Poole, and I had met the firm's owner, Ronald Nierop. Brian, who did not know that my seagoing notions had progressed from Stage One (the solo transatlantic race) to Stage Two (the circumnavigation), told me that Westfield had a Kingfisher 30

which was to be delivered to the United States. It was called
Dytiscus III . . . .

Dytiscus III was twelve months old, a former demonstration
boat designed for family use. When I was with Mr Nierop, it had
not occurred to me to ask about using it for going round the world.
I had got it into my head that round-the-world boats had to be
something new and something special, something purpose-built for
the battering which awaited them – and the months to come were to
show that this was one bit of sea-going theory on which I could not
be faulted. All the same, I had not wanted to turn up my untutored
nose too soon, and then find myself without a boat of any
description.

I thought that in the event of my failing to find something in
which to circumnavigate I would at least still be able to take part
in the tilt across the Atlantic.

And now, with my search falling apart at the seams, I began
to wonder if there would be a hope of my obtaining this very boat
and pushing it into the biggest test to which an ordinary production
boat could ever be subjected. At the January boat show in London,
Bill Ridley and I looked at a Kingfisher 30, identical in every way
to *Dytiscus III*. I had to air my doubts about the practicability of the
thing I was proposing. Bill listened sympathetically but stayed
non-committal. He does not claim to be a yachtsman and he is the
sort of character who will not pretend to know what he does not
know.

I found myself turning back to Neville Wood, whom I had by
now begun to regard as a sort of oracle of ocean-going. At his home,
fortified as usual by Wynne's coffee, I put *Dytiscus* up for judgment.
Neville was silent for a moment or two. Then :

'Those bilge keels', he said. 'I think they may be your biggest
problem. Most of your sailing will consist of running before the
wind, a great deal of it gale force in the roaring forties. I don't
really know how well she'll run. I haven't had a lot of experience
with bilge keels, and I've had none at all in heavy weather.'

We visited the boat, which was sitting in Poole Harbour and looking very smart with its red hull and grey deck. Mike Parry, buyer
with Westfield Engineering, showed us over.

Neville was still not keen on those bilge keels, which are designed
to enable the boat to stand upright if it is left on a mud mooring
when the tide goes out. In any case, they were going to be a little

bit purposeless once I began following Chichester: the whole point
of the exercise was that I must not touch land. I could not help
recalling a day the previous summer when Neville, for all his
reservations, would have been glad of bilge keels. He had wanted
to show me what happens when you go aground, and he went
straight for a bank. He showed me, all right: the boat wedged so
firmly that we could not shift it. It lay on its side for six hours until
the tide came in.

Aboard *Dytiscus,* he did not allow his thoughts on bilge keels
to persuade him into stinting his praise for the workmanship which
had gone into the boat. After a painstaking, hour-long tour, which
made me realize yet again how much he knew and how much I
didn't, he pronounced his verdict.

'It's a terrifically strong boat, and all the fittings are the very
best quality. You haven't got a floating caravan here – but it *is*
designed as a family cruising boat: you must not forget that.'

That was good enough for me. If Neville was impressed, I was
going to look no further. The next move was to tell Ronald Nierop
the true extent of my plan and hope that he would agree.

He did not keep me in suspense.

'She's there if you want her – but don't go for going's sake.
Go only if you are happy with the design.'

I sent a one-word telegram to Maureen: 'Yes.'

                                    * * * * * *

It was early February, 1968. Obtaining a boat had taken nearly
four months. I now had roughly the same amount of time in which
to have *Dytiscus III* modified in accordance with the expert advice
I was intent on obtaining; in which to list and obtain the necessary
supplies of food, drugs and equipment; in which to try to learn
something about navigation.

The time factor was important. Everything had to be calculated
with a view to my avoiding being at Cape Horn in the winter. The
best time to be there, if you feel you have to be there at all, is about
January or February, and I had decided to base my reckoning on the
plan adopted by Sir Francis Chichester, who had set off in August,
1966, in a bigger, faster boat, after spending a long time on the
planning stage. Neville Wood and I decided that it would be
necessary for me to leave earlier in the year than he had done,
because of the great difference between our boats, so we plumped

for July.

I knew that John Ridgway was hoping to start in June or July. But then, in March, John said he would be off some time in June. From then on, I knew I had to leave in June as well. After all, whether I filled in an entry form or not, publicity was turning the thing into a race. And if it was going to be a race I could not afford to give him several weeks' start — whatever weather I might be letting myself in for in the forties.

Two nights after Ronald Nierop had given me the go-ahead, I was in among the experts. I had enlisted the help of Frank Allen, a member of the Royal Southern Yacht Club, which I was to join two months later; Bill Cottell, a flag officer with the club and an ocean racer who had competed in the Bermuda race and other events; and Charlie Brooker, the foreman at Ian Proctor Metal Masts, of Bursledon, who was going to be responsible for modifications to the mast and rigging. We all met at Frank's house at Bursledon, six miles from Southampton, and discussed my plan.

The next day, the four of us made the pilgrimage to Poole. *Dytiscus* was in the factory yard, and I stood alongside the bilge keels that nobody seemed to love while the other three subjected the long-suffering boat to yet another searching examination, similar to that undertaken by Neville a few days earlier. My three experts on board were going their separate ways and shouting over the side every time they spotted something which they thought would need modifying. The trouble was, their requirements were quite extraordinarily nautical. I did not know what they were talking about, but I doggedly recorded their every wish in barely legible pencil on a piece of paper and felt sure that with so much applied science everything would simply have to work out right in the end. Bill noticed that the rudder was not properly aligned. A bearing was found to be badly worn, so it was stripped down later. This in turn led to the discovery of a badly corroded pin which would never have lasted the trip. What I would have done without the enthusiasm of my experts, I just don't know.

I made several such visits, and Brian Cooke was added to my team of advisers. He told me: 'If I was going, I would have to find out how she runs in a force nine.' At the time, knowing nothing of the ways of a sailing boat, I could not appreciate the significance of his words. Understanding was to come six months later, when finding out was entirely unavoidable.

Naturally, I wanted to learn all I could about the way the boat was put together : that at least would be something of a consolation if I had to set off in her without knowing anything about sailing. And I did, in fact, learn a lot. But I also wanted to make sure that by the time I crossed the starting line both the boat and myself were just as fully equipped as we possibly could be. This was why I set about adding to my detailed lists under such headings as navigation, clothing, diet, medical, radio, safety, cooking, spares and photography; this was why I made a point of going over my lists with all my knowledgeable friends individually, to see if they could think of anything I had forgotten; this was why, by June 8, I must have been the most comprehensively furnished non-sailor ever to have pointed a sharp-ended boat at an unsuspecting ocean.

I made another list, headed Factors. It contained seventeen of them, starting with yacht and finished with insurance, and taking in such things as seamanship, sailing experience, code words and clothing. Factor number eleven, sandwiched between Water and Mortgage, was . . . Maureen! The Diplomatic Corps would have shown me the door, and no questions asked.

I didn't do too well, either, on a list headed Plan. It was only five items strong, and the first three turned out to be beyond me. They went :

1. Maximum experience at sailing.
2. Learn navigation.
3. Qualify for solo transatlantic race (solo 500 miles).

Fortunately, at the time I made my plan, I did not know that the short answers to those three proposals would prove to be :

1. Six miles solo.
2. Oh, yeah?
3. See 1 and 2 above.

The work of preparing me and the boat went ahead. Frank Allen had the mast and rigging delivered on one of his coal lorries to Charlie Brooker's back garden at Bursledon. Charlie said the mast would need twin tracks for booms when running under twin head-sails. Frank said the sliding hatches on the cabin roof and the aft compartment should be sealed down in case they were carried away by a breaking wave. The forward anchor compartment was filled with foam to make a watertight bulkhead and reduce the possibility of my sinking if I failed to avoid an iceberg, despite having the whole world to aim at. The engine was removed. So was the toilet : I needed the space. A thirty-gallon water tank went where the engine had been.

Lee-boards and nets were fitted to the bunks. The boards – which I was surprised to find were not boards at all, but canvas – were to hold me in, and the nets were to hold my equipment, because each bunk would have to double as sleeping and storage space, depending on where the wind was coming from. Westfield Engineering did some of the work; we did the rest.

I did interesting things like learning to take one of my own teeth out. I never did discover how I was supposed to cope if I asked for gas . . . .

I did other interesting things, like confronting yacht chandlers' storemen with lists of equipment which I had been assured was necessary but whose particular function had not been disclosed to me. If the man behind the counter could not meet my specific demand, he would begin asking technical questions with the idea of offering me a substitute. This was my clue to disappear with the urgency of a schoolboy who has just learned it is bathnight.

'Got to go', I would say. 'Parking meter.'

Maureen, meanwhile, had lists of her own. She was my built-in quartermaster, responsible for buying food and arranging menus. Shopping for a year's food is quite an undertaking. Maureen did her job the only way she knows – thoroughly. I wanted a daily ration of four thousand calories, with a different menu for each day of the week. I never had cause to complain about either the food or its variety.

Mauren was responsible, too, for my 'special' packs. Tinned grouse for August 12, tinned pheasant for Christmas, tinned partridge for our anniversary, tinned haggis and some whisky for Burns' Night; and for my 'boredom parcels', which were likely to contain just about anything.

I had to do my best with the imponderables of navigation. Every time I had a free night, I would go to Neville's home. I would drop with the minimum of difficulty into my stuffed fish routine as he talked of longitudes and latitudes, of Greenwich mean time, local mean time and local apparent time, of noon sights and spherical triangles. *Spherical triangles?* I floundered without a pause and reached for some more of Wynne's coffee.

Eventually, however, a light began to dawn. I found I was able to work out the problems he gave me – but I had never actually done it in practice. So I took a couple of sights one day when I was out with Frank, and I took them home to work them out. They were both wrong. Then Neville took me just outside Portsmouth harbour. I took a sight and when we returned we worked it out together. It indicated that I had been just outside Portsmouth harbour. This was progress. This was my first cause for confidence.

By now, I had been out of the Army for several months – but I was still giving lectures, dozens of them. Their subject was different, however : it was now the Atlantic row. At one lecture, I met Cdr Meyers, of the Royal Navy's navigation school – *H.M.S. Dryad* – at Portsmouth. He lent me some books and gave me the chance of studying the Navy's approach to astronomical navigation, which involves finding your position by taking a sight of the sun and using time accurately. It was laid out a little differently from Neville's. I decided the best thing I could do was to work out a sort of compromise lay-out of my own.

I continued to concentrate on astro, despite being very much aware that I did not know how the tide tables worked and that I did not know about working with buoys or what navigation lights meant. Neville's theory, which I agreed seemed reasonable enough, was that I was not going to see any buoys or many lights and that I could teach myself all about them when I got to sea. It did mean that once I had left I could not enter a harbour because I would have been baffled by the buoyage system – but time was against me and my main concern was to try to avoid getting lost.

Eventually, *Dytiscus* was taken in a yacht transporter from Poole to a yacht chandler at Swanwick, on the Hamble. It was two weeks later than we had planned, but it could not be helped. The boat was put in the water alongside Frank's *Blue Crystal,* and the mast was stepped : that was one of my recently acquired nautical terms, and I suppose it sounds better than 'pushed in and stood upright', which was how I would have described the procedure until a few months previously. Fitting-out could begin.

About a quarter of a mile ahead, John Ridgway's *English Rose IV* was also being fitted out. I still had not told John of my plans, with the result that my efforts to avoid his spotting me were like something out of a pantomime. I could see him at work from my boat, but he did not have to see me.

I hope I was not being unduly juvenile. My reasoning seemed

quite sound at the time, and it was based on the fact that John
and I had come through a lot together : nine years in the Parachute
Regiment and three months in a rowing boat. We knew each other's
strengths and weaknesses, and the basic difference between us is
that John does not share my perennial optimism.

He has a more comprehensive appreciation of the fact that life
is real and life is earnest. This was why his yacht was being reinforced and fitted with special equipment. If I had told him that
I was bent on the same undertaking in a twelve-month-old family
class boat, he would have begun asking the sort of questions which
would have sowed in me the seeds of doubt, especially when I was
unable to come up with satisfactory answers. So I kept out of John's
way and said nothing. When one of John's helpers spotted me after
a few days, John asked what I was doing, and I said I was thinking
about getting ready for the solo transatlantic race. And when my
first set of sails was delivered by mistake to the yard where *English
Rose IV* was being worked on, my arrival to collect them led to my
collecting some funny looks as well. Stoutly, I said nothing.

I still had to find out what was going to happen when I took
Dytiscus out without anyone to supervise me. I decided to have a
week's sailing at Langstone, so Neville came on board and Frank
towed me from the Hamble with *Blue Crystal*. I chose the wrong
week : every day was virtually calm, and my only venture 'outside'
was that visit to the Nab Tower – which put any more solo practice
out of the question because it ended with my wrenching a muscle in
my right arm when I made a botch of my first attempt at mooring
unaided to a buoy. The boat was going too fast. I leaned over to the
buoy, grabbed the mooring line, failed to wrap it round the cleat, and
was misguided enough to think I could stop nine tons of yacht by
simply holding on . . . .

The preparations went on. At one of my lectures, I met Trevor
Starr, a metallurgist. He checked my self-steering gear and told me
about the problems of dissimilar metals.

John Deacon's Sailor Marine radio was to be fitted when *Dytiscus*
was taken to Chris Waddington's Wicor Marine, at Porchester,
for the final stages of the work. While Maureen spent her evenings
knitting extra sweaters and two balaclava helmets – one of which
she gave to John – I was sitting in my bedroom tuning in to various
beacons on a borrowed receiver which had a radio direction finder,
so that I could practise plotting them. And I had a week in the

B

Honda factory, stripping and assembling an engine – which was what I might have to do if my generator broke down.

Maureen and I had promised ourselves a fortnight's holiday in Scotland. It shrank by stages until we were lucky to have five days, and even then we spent a great deal of time on chart work. She never complained. Neville supervised the work on *Dytiscus* while we were away.

When we returned on May 3, there was still a frightening amount to be done. I felt sure it would be impossible to start on June 1, the date we had set ourselves, and I wanted to put it off for a month. It was Bil Ridley who talked me out of that idea.

'Let's try to meet our target', he said. 'Then we shall only be a bit behind. If we put it back we shall relax and slow down. We must keep up the pace.'

He was right. In the end, we were just a week late.

I had to pass *English Rose IV* when I was driving to Frank Allen's house at Bursledon to collect his speedometer, mile recorder and sextant, which he was lending me as spares. This reminded me that I still had not told John. Over dinner on May 5, I did so.

As I had foreseen, he did not think I should go ahead – but by this time there could be no turning back. A fortnight later, John left the Hamble to sail to the Aran Isles. I went to wish him luck and I gave him one of the two St. Christophers which had come with us across the Atlantic.

John left the Aran Isles on June 1, the day I had hoped to start. Maureen and I sent him a cable : 'Who dares, wins. Who cares who wins? Last home's a cissy. We will be following you.'

We received no reply. John had other things on his mind by then.

I had plenty to think about, too. I had myself measured for a special dirty weather suit, which I was told was under consideration by the Board of Trade and the White Fish Authority, obtained a tape recorder, signed contracts, passed my medicals, had a haircut, made my will . . . .

Each evening, I would go over the navigation with Neville. I was with him on the boat at 2 a.m. on Thursday, June 6, two days before I sailed, listening to time signals after a four-hour session with the charts. How do you express your gratitude for friendship like that? The previous morning, Maureen and her sister, Christine, came with me to the boat for its blessing by Father Brennan.

Then, of course, there was the packing. The food went into a polytheen bag, a day's rations to a bag. Each bag was put into another bag and heat-sealed. Five days' rations then went into a large polythene coal bag provided by Frank Allen. Again, we heat-sealed. A neighbour, and ex-paratrooper, Eric Downey, lent us a bedroom for storage until we could start to load the boat, once he had realized we were in danger of packing ourselves right out through the windows.

We began transferring the parcels to *Dytiscus* on Monday, June 3. We were on the final lap.

With the approach of D (for *Dytiscus*) *Day*, I was becoming increasingly aware of my responsibilities to the Royal Southern Yacht Club. It was there that I was to start from, and I did not want to embarrass the club by getting the entire proceedings wrapped firmly round my neck. That was why Bill Cottell and Frank Allen had arranged for me to meet Ken Purser, the Club Commodore. I felt I had a duty to confess my inadequacies at the same time as I asked for the club's co-operation. The four of us had gone into the committee room one evening in early May, and I had told him I was intending to sail round the world.

'Tremendous!' Ken said. 'I wish you had told me sooner. I should have liked to have done something to help.'

'Ken', I said. 'You still can. There's a small problem. I can't sail.'

There was one of those silences. Ken looked at Frank. Frank looked at Bill. Bill loked back at Ken. And Ken give him his due, took it well. He blinked a bit, naturally, but I was not going to blame him for that.

'That's all right', he said. 'We shall have to make a plan.'

'Ken', I said fervently, 'I've already made one . . . ."

The scheme was that Frank, in *Blue Crystal*, would tow *Dytiscus* into position behind the starting line. With me would be Neville Wood, Chris Waddington and Frank's fifteen-year-old son, Timothy, who were going to see to the sails and self-steering gear for me; besides Maureen and baby Samantha, ready for the goodbyes.

Ken, aboard his boat, *Samantha IV*, was to fire the starting gun the moment I crossed the line – as the signal that I had started and most definitely *not* as the signal for me to start : I had visions of the gun going off, and then an idotic hiatus while I manoeuvred frantically to try to make the boat go the way it was supposed to go.

Once I was set sail, the others would leave me. Maureen, Samantha and Timothy would transfer to Frank's boat; Chris and Neville each to his own; Neville would get ahead of me as quickly as he could, and I would watch him like a hawk: everything he did to his sails, I would do to mine. This was the only hope I had of getting out of Southampton Water, turning right and heading down the Solent without trying conclusions with the Isle of Wight. And Frank would stay behind me in *Blue Crystal,* ready to head off any other boats which threatened to come too close to me because their owners did not suspect that I had no idea of how to avoid them.

'Ken', I said, 'there's one other thing. I shall be grateful if you will ask any club members who accompany me not to come any further than the Needles. That's where Neville will have to leave me to get back to his pupils, so God know what will happen after that.'

Again, Ken reassured me.

Our meeting over, I left the clubhouse and looked hard along the watery way I was to go. I tried not to think of what Rabbie Burns had been moved to say about mice and the rest of us.

* * * * * *

Reveille on D Day at Blyth Mansion was 0600 hours. It was a house full of women: my wife, my mother-in-law, my sister Isobel, my sister-in-law Christine, and baby Sammy, who was not quite eleven months old. Chaos! Women dashing everywhere. Christine trying to separate Colonel, our labrador, from Judy, her Yorkshire terrier. Me not helping matters by giving them a countdown every ten minutes and saying if they were not ready I should have to go anyway, or I would miss the tide.

0800 hours. Phone Chris Waddington and find that a rope we are waiting for has not arrived. Phone a yacht chandler's and arrange to pick one up on the way to the Hamble.

0830 hours. Everybody into the car. I can't believe it. We are stacked up with flasks of soup and boxes of sandwiches, so that I will not have to bother about cooking for my first few hours aboard. Cooking? Who can face food? At breakfast, I had recoiled palely from the steak which Maureen had put in front of me, and sought refuge in five cups of black coffee.

Need some exercise books for my personal log, which is to be written with the silver propelling pencil Frank and Audrey Allen gave me at dinner last night. Stop at Fareham outside stationer's. Double yellow lines. Risk it. Re-emerge and promise interested policeman that I will not do such a thing again for a long time.

More coffee at the club, with the commodore and officers, Mr and Mrs Nierop, and others who have helped.

See Bill Ridley. Did you get that cine camera, Bill? Wonder what he sighed like that for . . . ?

Goodbye, goodbye, goodbye, goodbye. Hell, he's got a handshake: glad I'm not the Duke . . . .

I'm aboard. This is it. Chay Blyth will now make a fool of himself. Ropes everywhere. Better look busy. Can't even raise the bloody burgee. Chris to the rescue. Why didn't it jam for him?

Everybody's leaving me. Maureen kisses me, presses a St Christopher into my hand. We'll be praying for you.

Bye-bye, baby Sam. If I can't find Madeira, I'll come straight back.

Neville says: 'Don't starve the sails, and keep her on the port tack. I will catch up before you transfer to the starboard tack . . . ."

I pray that he will. God, how I pray that he will.

And now they've gone, and the boat's sailing itself.

Bang!

That's it: the moment it's all been about. What a feeling. All we need now is a notice on the front: 'Look out, world, I don't know where my brakes are.' Hope to God that after all this I don't hit France.

Bloody fool! Bloody, bloody fool!

Take your hands out of your pockets!

Now, then, what's Neville doing up front?

3

Backroom Girl

Maureen Blyth

*L*ITTLE shivers kept taking me by surprise as I stood on the
deck of Frank Allen's boat with Samantha in my arms watching
this unpredictable husband of mine making hopeful overtures
to his sails while he preceded us up the Solent; but my shivers were
nothing to do with the temperature. They were the shivers of
uncertainty which had arrived with the realization that this was the
day that everything else had been all about. The matter-of-factness
of the months of preparation had suddenly been replaced by the
pell-mell panic of committing my man to the water. We had taken
the ultimate, irrevocable step, and somehow it was only now that the
enormity of our presumption was dawning on me; only now, that
the implications of that little red boat fifty yards ahead were starting
to chase butterflies round my tummy; only now, that the sudden
reality of watching the novice sailor-boy swishing towards the
unknown was giving me niggling doubts about the practicability
of it all.

I think Audrey suspected the turmoil which was inside me. She
stood with me at intervals, the breeze winnowing through the tuft
of hair which had escaped from beneath her woolly hat, and offered
a gentle reassurance. 'Chay's no fool.' Or else, 'Trust Chay. It won't
take him long to find out how to go about things.'

In my heart of hearts, I believed she was right. Chay, I told
myself, was certainly no fool. Crazy, maybe; but certainly no fool.
He had prepared for The Big Trip, which was the way we had
adopted of describing it, with an unswerving insistence that when
he set off he would set off as fully prepared as it was possible to be.
His aim was to overlook no detail, however small; to get advice
and help from people best qualified to give it; and to take on himself the responsibility for final decisions whenever it was necessary
for decisions to be made.

The bald fact of his trying to go round the world non-stop in the wrong type of yacht, with no practical navigation knowledge and his solo sailing experience limited to a six-mile trip and a short haul round the harbour, made him sound crazy by any standards – but at least it was a calculated craziness, with every possible step taken to foresee the likely snags and eventualities. And perhaps this time he was going to get this adventurous streak of his out of his system : perhaps, if he achieved his non-stop goal, he would settle down so that we could start having the sort of married life that other people had – a married life where planning for the future meant thinking about things for home and family, rather than getting all wound up in one unlikely adventure after another.   Admittedly, I would much rather have an adventurous man than a man tied to a nine-to-five existence, because I hate routine, too – but when I got Chay Blyth I had no idea just how far from routine I was going to be taken in my role of backroom girl in the task of challenging life the Chay way.

The day that was to change my life was a day in May, 1962. I was eighteen, a private in the Queen Alexandra Nursing Corps, and I was sitting with a group of girls at an afternoon dance at Aldershot, where I had been posted the previous day after completing my training at Hindhead, Surrey. At a table nearby were a group of young soldiers, but apart from registering that one of them – a noisy, chunky, cheerful character with a Scots accent you could hang your hat on – was gorgeously tanned and just a bit inebriated, I did not really take any notice of them. Then, however, this same soldier came shambling over, looked me as squarely in the eye as he could, and asked me to dance with him.

'No, thank you', I said.

'Please get up and dance.'

It was not so much a request as a command. I got up, followed his stocky frame into a clearing on the floor, and spent the next three minutes marvelling at the insistence with which he was trying to make sense out of what was obviously a foreign art.

'What are you doing tomorrow night?'

He shouted the question above the noise of the record which was accompanying the enormous expenditure of energy to which he had by this time committed himself. I said I did not know.

'Will you come out with me, then?'

The tone of the question indicated that there was no thought that I would say anything but Yes. I hedged.

'I don't know.'

'I'll see you at seven, outside the Pegasus.'

'I'm not sure . . . .'

'I'll be there. Seven o'clock.'

I was still not sure, and I told my girl friends so when the record had finished and I had been brusquely herded back to my table. Back in his own group, the Scotsman – who, I was to learn, had returned from a tour of duty in the Persian Gulf two days previously – was getting down to the serious business of ordering another round of drinks. We all looked at him surreptitiously. Go on, Maureen –he's probably not a bad chap . . . .

So I went – but I made a point of going five minutes later than the time he had specified. He was standing outside the Pegasus, which is one of the pubs adopted by the Parachute Regiment as its rendezvous in Aldershot, and I tucked myself into a cinema doorway on the other side of the road and watched him for a moment or two. I convinced myself that he looked pretty reasonable and I decided to go through with it. And that was the decision which turned out to be the one that mattered. Seven months later, on Christmas Eve, 1962, we were married.

Most of the time we were courting, Chay was away on exercises and things, and I did not really have much opportunity to find out about his attitude to adventure until after we were married. I suppose I should have suspected that I had drawn something of a surprise packet, really, because two months before our first meeting he had taken part in his first canoe race – which just happened to be the longest canoe race in the world, a hundred-and-twenty-five miles, Devizes to Westminster.

Once we were married, however, it began to dawn on me that I was not seeing an awful lot of this boy of mine because he always seemed to be off canoeing or climbing, or doing something equally outdoor and physical. But the awareness grew slowly. It was not just thrown at me. And I came to accept that life with Chay meant for considerable periods life without Chay. By the time he began talking about rowing the Atlantic with John Ridgway, in April, 1966, I had been conditioned for three-and-a-half years to the fact of having a husband who insisted on chasing challenges.

On reflection, it seems odd when I say that the prospect of letting my husband go off on the most impossible piece of oarsmanship ever contemplated did not frighten me. Not that there was really any question of my *letting* him go : Chay is the sort of man you do not question. He was not the type you would want to stop doing anything. I would not want to change him, even if I knew how to. Having Chay for a husband ensures that squaring up to uncertainty becomes in itself a way of life – and, of course, it does wonders for your geography. And when it became apparent that the only thing I could be certain of in the immediate future was the prospect of having a husband who was stuck in a ridiculous little boat somewhere in the middle of the Atlantic, I accepted it as I had accepted everything else – more or less as a matter of course.

I got to know about it only about a month before he was leaving, which did not really give me much time to dwell on it. But I think the reason I was not frightened was that I could not grasp the immensity of the project – probably because Chay had never been to sea before and could not tell me anything about what was likely to happen.

And I remembered that whatever he had set out to do in the past he had always completed successfully – which I know did not really have any bearing on it, but somehow or other it was a very consoling thought.

But although I was not frightened, I was worried. I had a feeling – which proved to be correct – that once he had gone I would have a lot of sleepless nights. But I did not attempt to dissuade him, because I could not see the point of trying. If I had managed to talk him out of it, John would have gone in any case, with a different partner, and there was the possibility that Chay would have said, 'I could have been there . . . .''

My view is that if your number is up, your number is up – whether you are rowing the Atlantic or crossing the road. The way Chay puts it is that when he goes he wants to go straight through the front door : no back entrance for him. And I would much rather have him killed doing something he enjoyed doing – or, at least, something he wanted to do : I do not think I have ever heard him say that he actually *enjoyed* the Atlantic, although I suppose in his own way he must have done. I have never heard him say that he did not enjoy it, either. His attitude has always been that if someone asked him to go again he would refuse – but that he would go if he had not already done it.

With Chay, the important thing is doing something the first

time and finding out what sort of effect it has on him. Testing the human frame is his idea of a good time, and I knew this before he began to talk about doing the Atlantic.

All the same, my opinion was the same as everybody else's : that the pair of them were mad. But the factor on which I was basing my judgment was the sheer distance – it turned out to be three thousand five hundred miles – they were proposing to row, rather than the conditions under which that rowing would be done. The idea that they would be facing a hurricane in a twenty-foot rowing boat never entered my head. When Chay was away, I was worried because he was away, not because of what he was going through. And when he came back and told me all about it, I still did not appreciate the full implications of what he had done. Never having been to sea myself, I just could not imagine the nightmare of that crazy journey. Thus it was that the Atlantic, which had crept quietly into my life, had remained with me, accepted as just another manifestation of what life with Chay was all about.

And this present enterprise had not come as a shock, either. It had sneaked up on me gradually for something like twelve months, gently developing from the days when Chay was doing nothing more than express an objective admiration for Sir Francis. I was living with the sea all the time that my husband was considering the possibilities of entering the Single-Handed Transatlantic Race, which was due to begin in June, 1968, and it seemed almost the most natural thing in the world when his target switched to going round the globe non-stop. The thing with Chay is that once he starts talking about something which really appeals to him he seems to talk so much that by the time he has passed his ideas over to you you begin to think they are your own ideas, and you have accepted them before you realise what is happening.

During that car ride to Hawick, our conversation moved from the Transatlantic race to Sir Francis's achievement and then, all of a sudden, we were sailing round the world non-stop and I was there as well, chipping in with ideas on how it could be done. From that moment onwards, we never discussed the Transatlantic race. The only times we mentioned it were when we told people that that was what Chay was aiming for. But between ourselves it was always The Big Trip.

Admittedly, when Chay began actually looking for a boat it drove the reality of his idea home a stage further – to the stage, in fact, where we were even going to sell the bungalow and the furniture in order to raise the money. And it was at this time that I went into one of my turmoils of uncertainty. I was praying and praying he would get what he wanted – and I was also praying and praying that he *would not* get what he wanted. I simply did not know what I was praying for. Then a telegram boy come walking down the garden path with a telegram which just said 'Yes', and I broke down and cried. The uncertainty was over. There could be no backing out.

Once, however, that I had had time to think it over, I was quite relieved about it. It meant that it would not be long before he was away –and the sooner he was away, the sooner he would be back. Back, I hoped, to stay. Every night, after a day of scrubbing the boat or packing parcels or dashing to London to pick up a sextant or compass, I would pray that he was going to achieve his goal. I felt that if he succeeded he would settle down. Probably, this was why I helped him a lot more than I needed to, doing things which he could have done himself – just to help as much as possible, thinking that if we put everything into it he was bound to be successful and that this would be the last time.

People talked to me about the sacrifices I was making. I do not think I made any sacrifices, unless you counted a lack of sleep. I do not like losing my sleep because it makes me feel like fighting my own shadow. But as for giving up time and the odd little luxuries, that is what you are married for : that is what you are there for. And there were always the moments of laughter to help things along – like the time we were preparing to pack a vast quantity of Batchelor's Vesta foodpacks into Frank Allen's polythene coal bags. We were sitting on the living room floor, in front of the fireplace, opening the cartons and removing the individual packets they contained, putting the cartons on one side of us and the packets on the other. I do not know how long we had been working when we suddenly became aware of the landscape we were creating : empty cardboard boxes were spreading out across the carpet and threatening to climb the chimney in a huge pile, three feet high. The sheer absurdity of it made us roar.

And there was the night which was to lead to Chay's having a radio telephone – the night of January 16, when John Deacon called to take him to give a talk at Southampton. Chay was wearing the dirty old shirt and trousers in which he had arrived home from his work at his motor body repair garage, and the pair of us were on

our hands and knees, poring over charts which were spread all over
the floor. There was a dong from the doorbell, which sent us into
an immediate frenzy of effort to hide the evidence : the fewer people
who knew of The Big Trip, the better. I went to the window and
peered through the curtain, which I parted only fractionally, feeling
like Agent XYZ taking a furtive peep at a foreign keyhole.

'Chay, it's a man.'

'What's he look like?'

He barked the question as he bundled a pile of papers behind
cushions and into drawers and pounced on some more.

'He's very tall . . . I haven't seen him before.'

'Let's have a look . . . .'

But Chay did not know him either, so we returned with even
more anxiety to the task of tidying up. After what seemed an age,
I went to the door. Our visitor, a fair-haired six-footer, broad-
shouldered and upright in a dark overcoat, announced his name and
his mission. I showed him into the living room and broke the news
to Chay.

'Chay, this is Mr Deacon. Did you know you're supposed to be
giving a lecture to the Southampton Lions tonight?'

'Tonight?' Chay did not have to say more. It was quite obvious
that he did not know. But as John Deacon promptly pointed out,
there was no reason why he should have known : he had been
given an altogether different date by mistake when the arrangement
was made. The trouble was, there were at this moment something
like fifty people sitting down to dinner twenty-seven miles away
and expecting to hear a talk about the *English Rose* when the meal
was finished.

'God Lord ' Chay said. 'I'll get washed and changed straight
away.'

He shot off to the bathroom, and I invited our visitor to sit
down while I made him a cup of coffee.

'No, thank you, if you don't mind : I must make a telephone
call.'

'Oh . . . I'm afraid we haven't got a phone here, but there's
a kiosk not far away. You have to go . . . .'

'No, that's all right : there's a phone in my car.'

He smiled good-humouredly as he saw me blink. I showed him
out of the door again, then raced round to find Chay some clean
underwear and a shirt. When Mr Deacon returned, I asked him

how long it would take to get to Southampton.

'Between twenty-five and thirty minutes, I should think.'

'Good heavens, you must have a fast car!'

'Not really : a Rolls Royce.'

Again, he smiled with a complete absence of pretension. A Rolls Royce! And a few minutes ago I had offered him a plebeian cup of coffee. I resolved to redress the balance.

'Ai say! Would you like a whisky before you go?'

He shook his head, then I left him in order to find out if there was anything I could do to help Chay, who was in our bedroom. 'Chay', I said, 'do you realise you are going to Southampton in a Rolls Royce?' He peered through the blind, and there it was, parked outside in the January night.

A minute or two afterwards, I was seeing them off at the front door. Chay grinned. 'Pity it isn't light enough for the neighbours to see – but we'd better walk slowly down the path because somebody may be peeping out of a window.'

After they had gone, I closed the door and stood for a moment with my back to it. God, I thought, he must think we're a couple of nutters.

When Chay returned – having been chauffeured this time by John Deacon's son, David – and told me that he had been offered a radio telephone for a boat he still had not obtained, I was as astounded as he was. I had not worried at the thought of Chay's going round the world without a radio. I had been oddly confident that he would not run into trouble, and I had not been concerned that I would not receive telegrams because I thought he would be meeting ships so that I would get letters instead. I did not think twice about it because my view was that if Chay was going off on a trip like this one I simply had to be prepared for the long silences which must necessarily be the result of the intervals between his encountering ships. And even if he did not manage to get a letter on board, he would have been able to hoist his MIK – the three-flag signal which means 'report me to Lloyds' – so it was not as if he were going to be entirely cut off from the world.

All the same, when Chay came home and told me that a radio had suddenly become a possibility, I was as thrilled and grateful as he was. It was a wonderful gesture, and one which gave a terrific spur to our hopes. We felt that things were going our way at last.

As the preparations went on, I became so absorbed in them and in trying to digest Chay's various instructions and requirements, that I just did not seem to have any personal reactions or feelings at all.

Everything was geared to the task of bringing him face to face once again with his old friend Survival, with whom he had established this odd love-hate relationship. I am sure he does not enjoy having to cook for himself and having nobody to talk to. But it means a lot to him when he comes back and finds he has not gone cuckoo and can still carry on an intelligent conversation at the end of a couple of months.

The preparations included the discovery that nobody was going to insure him without a colossal premium. 'Ah, yes, Mr Blyth. You are intending to sail round the world without stopping. What sailing experience do you have, Mr Blyth?

'You've been round Langstone Harbour and out to the Nab Tower. I see . . . .

'Miss Jones, will you show Mr Blyth out, please?" '

This did not worry me. I had been working up to the time of Samantha's birth, and I was young enough to start working again if necessary. I was more concerned with the task of getting my dear, crazy husband off on his adventure as fully prepared as he could possibly be, whether he was insured or not. While Chay was trying to learn something about sailing and navigation, I was doing my duties as quartermaster, secretary and errand-girl. I had a great deal of help from Jan Kinch, our next-door neighbour. She did a lot of typing for us, and if I had to rush off suddenly to collect something vital for the voyage she would look after Samantha for me.

Chay's special packs and 'boredom parcels' were my idea. I knew he would have times when anything different would be welcome, so I used to hunt round the shops and find little things that I thought could be pushed in. I got one of his sisters, Isobel, in Hawick, to send me about two dozen little Highland Toffee bars, which he absolutely loves. They are just chunks of gooey toffee, intended for children, but he thinks they are marvellous.

When we first started planning, it was agreed that he would take tapes with messages on them from Samantha and me and Mummy and all sorts of people. But suddenly he changed his mind and said he did not want any messages at all. He thought it might upset him. So my new instructions were simply to fill the tapes with music from long-playing records and leave it at that.

Taping time was when Samantha was up in Newcastle for a fortnight with Mummy. I set myself up in the bedroom, mainly because the bedroom was about the only place in the bungalow we could get into. Everywhere else was full of special clothing and equipment, and the piles of food which I had been accumulating. I put the record player on a chair and the tape recorder on the bed with all the records I was going to need for the immediate session, and before making a start I would always take the bedside telephone – we got a telephone soon after Mr Deacon's visit – off the hook. Unfortunately, I could not immobilze the front door bell, so a few of my fifteen recorded programmes contained an unexpected bing-bong-bing-bong. Whenever the bell went, I would creep to the front door as quickly and as quietly as I could, open the door, put my finger to my lips, and say 'Ssssh!' My visitors obviously assumed that the strain of it all was beginning to tell.

I did not manage to get all the tapes done before Samantha was back home, so one or two of my later ones contained unintentional reproductions of S.F. at full squeal. And one tape had a little message from me, squeezed in on the spur of the moment in defiance of the skipper's orders, with something from Dusty Springfield to follow.

Among all his other preoccupations – his sailing, his navigation, his planning, his medical checks – Chay did not neglect the most important factor of all : himself. For the last two months of his preparations, he ran four miles, first thing in the morning – through a wood and across fields and past a golf course and back past the outskirts of the estate. When he went, I had an extra ten minutes in bed, then I got up and had his bath running by the time he arrived home to do his press-ups in the back garden. He always came back in the filthiest condition, with mud everywhere, but one day his red track suit was in an even worse state than usual – as a result of stepping into what he thought was a small puddle and finding too late that it was a knee-deep ditch.

To help things along, we borrowed a rowing machine from John Ridgway and installed it on a concrete patch outside the back door. Chay began using this odd-looking object, which was by no means the most modern of machines, with a simply frightful determination – heaving himself backwards and forwards and making the strangest grunting noises until I was sure the neighbours must have thought I was strangling him. Morning after morning, he put himself through purgatory.

Then came the disaster which had always seemed inevitable when I had considered the width of the rowing machine seat in relation to the width of Chay's: after a particularly determined heave, he shot straight off the side and landed in a hot and noisy heap on the concrete. That was the end of rowing exercises.

Now, as I watched *Dytiscus* carrying my intrepid adventurer on towards the Needles, which was where we would shout our final goodbyes, the memory of that moment chuckled to the surface. The months we had left behind were full of incidents like that; abounding in absurdies which had helped to ease the inevitably mounting tension attending the approach of today's launching. Indeed, on this very morning, the saga of the preparations in which so many friends had played so big a part had yielded yet another incident of preposterous impossibility.

It had been at 1 a.m., at the end of a farewell dinner party, that Chay had shattered Bill Ridley by saying: 'I've got another little job for you, Bill: can you get me a cine camera?'

It was typical Chay. He had grown so accustomed to tackling the impossible that he did not think twice about asking anybody else to do the same. The 'little job' he had just given Bill would have to be accomplished in the nine hours which remained before the scheduled departure time of 10 a.m. – and Bill's problem was that he and his wife and two children were staying in an hotel on Hayling Island, about thirty-five miles away.

With nine-year-old Sara and seven-year-old Marc in the back seat, Bill and Betty set off at 7 a.m. to drive to Southampton. All the way, they were peering into the windows of closed camera shops, looking for the camera they wanted.

At 8.15, when they were in Fareham, they spotted one – but the shop, like all the others, was not due to open for another three-quarters of an hour and time was precious. After a series of enquiries, Bill found a garage about a hundred yards away, the owner of which was able to tell him where the shopkeeper lived. Bill rang the shopkeper from a call box, explained what he wanted and why, and persuaded him to go to the shop and let him in. Bill examined the camera, said he would buy all the coloured film he had in stock to go with it, got ten per cent discount, and persuaded him to agree to accepting a cheque for well over a hundred pounds into the bargain. Considering that Bill was a complete stranger to the shopkeeper, it was a quite remarkable feat all round.

Bill and his family arrived at the Hamble at 9.45 a.m. and dashed down to the boat, where they found Chay ambling about while more skilled hands than his attended to the last-minute preparations.

'Hello, Bill. Did you get that cine camera . . . ?'

Bill took it very well. He and the other members of the team had got to know Chay pretty thoroughly by then. Those last few days, nobody had been in bed much before 2 a.m., after a day's work on the boat had been followed by about seven hours of packing rations into polythene bags.

At last, the preparations were over. Chay Blyth, the novice of the non-stop, was on his hopeful way.

Was I stupid to have let him go? There was no letting up about it, although he insisted that he would not have gone if I had said he could not. I was sure he would have gone in any case, having talked me into believing that it was all my idea in the first place. What a character!

And now we are turning about. It is four o'clock and we have reached the Needles. The day has already given my master mariner about twenty-five miles' sailing experience, which is four times the total he had when the starting gun went off. And now he's going round the world. Just like that.

Come on, Samantha. Wave to Daddy.

4

All at Sea

Chay Blyth: June 8 – June 25

THE flotilla left me gradually to my own devices. Frank Allen, Neville Wood and Chris Waddington were with me all the way to the Needles, watching my efforts to pretend to be a sailor and shouting the occasional word of advice or encouragement. But then it was time for the final waves, to them and to Maureen and little Samantha. I watched my expert friends turn about with the maximum of skill and the minimum of fuss, and I was aware of a little thrill of envy at their competence. I could not have accomplished such a manoeuvre so gracefully and efficiently. Not that this mattered: I was just the chap who was going to go round the world without stopping.

The enormity of what lay before me prompted a sudden panic. *Steady, Blyth! Even you should find it difficult to bump into the world now that the world has become a thing composed entirely of water.*

* * * * * *

It was a thought which in its turn raised the question of where I was. It was the first time I had sailed out of sight of land, and I did not find it a pleasant sensation. Unhappily, I realized it was time to put my navigational knowledge to the test. Even more unhappily, I discovered that my log – that is the little electrical device which projects through the hull and records your speed and the distance you cover – was not working properly. This mean that my dead reckoning, a doubtful quantity at the best of times, was out for the count in the first round. *Stone* dead reckoning, you might say. So I pinned by hopes to radio beacons and I failed irrefutably.

I tried to convince myself it was all nerves; that I could not concentrate; that I would settle down. Perhaps it was; perhaps I couldn't; perhaps I would. But that did not alter the essence of the matter one iota : I had been at sea eight hours, and I was lost.

My first prayer of the voyage came with no difficulty at all. Then I settled to an uneasy sleep.

Waking up the next morning did not solve my problem. It was obvious that I had wasted no time at all in getting into the sort of mess that my record in navigation had pointed to as being high on the list of probabilities. I was hoping to find my way round the world but I was lost in Lyme Bay. I had promised Maureen that I would return home if I could not find Madeira, which was about thirteen hundred miles along my route. Find Madeira? I could not even find England.

I stayed lost for two days, despite swinging north to go and look for England. The only consolation was my two calls to Maureen – although the second of them was a throat-lumping business.

Despite the handicap which I was to the voyage, I had been gradually getting further away from home, and I knew that that would be the last time for a long time that I would hear the voice of the girl who was backing her man in his harebrained hopes to the limit. I am sure the operator knew how I felt when he called me back to tell me the length of the call. It was like being severed from society. But not to worry : there was only about another year to go.

I had jumped firmly on Frank's idea, which Maureen had told me about over the radio, that he should arrange for a helicopter to ferry me another complete log. The papers would have loved that – and who could blame them? Know-Nothing Novice Gets Air Drop. I could see it now. No, I would settle for the log I was stuck with – the log which so far as I had been able to judge seemed to work only when the weather was a bit rough. I took it to pieces, swapped parts, fiddled with it in a spirit of diminishing faith, and then acknowledged that it was too clever for me.

The astro, however, seemed to be behaving itself, which was something, because every other approach to pinpointing my position turned out to be a bit abysmal. Radio beacons and dead reckoning did nothing for me – entirely, as I sadly realized, owing to my own shortcomings. Finding that all my Brazil nuts had gone bad was another – though lesser – disaster. I am a great nut-nibbler. I tossed them over the side and failed to cheer myself up with the thought that the only nut still on board was me.

June 13, my fifth day at sea, gave me a look at Ushant – and the first hint of the way *Dytiscus III* was likely to behave when the clerk of the weather really began to throw things at me. As the wind came up, I came down – first to jib and one reef in the mainsail, and eventually to the storm jib. The boat, as my advisers had feared, did not run too well at all under self-steering gear. She was yawing all over the place – but at this stage I did not know whether the cause was the boat, the gear, or Blyth; I was inclined to think it was probably me. Everything was trial and error. I was sure that if Sir Francis could come aboard to sort things out our progress would be considerably more impressive.

I was worried, too, by the awareness that all the wrongs I was presumably inflicting were being inflicted on somebody else's boat. If anything disastrous happened to *Dytiscus,* the Blyth conscience was going to be far from easy for a long time to come. Already, I was wishing that I had borrowed the money and bought the boat from Ronald Nierop instead of having been so quick to accept his willingness to take a chance with me.

The boat was beginning to rocket along before the wind, despite my efforts to slow down by playing out a warp – that is the two-hundred-foot long rope which was on board for that very purpose. The self-steering gear – its visible manifestation a vane above the stern, three feet six inches high and about two feet wide, and some lengths of rope to the tiller – was bothering me a little, too : it looked so fragile. I was not happy, either, about the spinner log which was trailing behind and recording the distance I was covering. I suspected that it might get tied up with the works.

Nevertheless, I felt I was beginning to know my way about the boat – even if it was only to the extent that I ceased to be surprised by the things I could do wrong. I was settling down in as much as I was becoming acclimatized to the mediocrity of my performance. Things, I began to think, could only improve. They did not, of course : next day started with my losing the shackle which linked the topping lift – that is another nautical word for a rope – to the boom; and it ended with my flashing my torch over the sails at 2300 hours in a desperate – and fortunately successful – bid to show a tanker that *Dytiscus* was not a motor boat before it mowed me down. Once it realised what sort of boat my navigation lights were attached to, it observed the rule of the water – that sails have right of way. And as the matinée performance I had the discovery that I was five gallons of water short in my water tank. That really was a blow – the more so, because Chris Waddington had said to me : 'Are your tanks full, or should we check them?' And I, true to my well nurtured habit of answering without thinking, had said : 'They're all right.'

What with one thing and another, I found myself doing some pretty solid thinking about the point of this extraordinary exercise which I had set myself – and for the life of me, I could not find it. Sir Francis had done the trip in a boat which must have cost at least twenty thousand pounds, and he had stopped at Australia for a re-fit. And here was I in a little family yacht costing five thousand pounds, proposing to do the thing without a halt. This was the exercise for which I had left Maureen at home with Samantha, who was now eleven months old. This was, surely, the ultimate demonstration of conceit and selfishness.

I thought : 'If I owned the boat, I would definitely turn round and go back.' But that was something I could not do when so many people had shown so much faith in me and had done so much to get me on my unseamanlike way. A little holiday in Ropelawshiel, the isolated cottage we had got in Selkirkshire on a ninety-nine year lease, had never seemed more attractive. I wondered when Maureen would begin the big decorating programme which she had planned as a way of taking her mind off her wandering boy. As if to rub things in, one of my batteries overflowed when I was charging it, leaving me to chase away the impressive consequences with lots of bicarbonate of soda. Bill Ridley had suggested that we ought to put the batteries in heavy-gauge polythene bags : that was another time when I had not thought carefully enough before replying.

And now there was no wind. It seemed that I could not strike the balance I needed. Either it blew me too hard or it just packed up and went home. I began to feel that if I completed the trip it would take me roughly two years. I was more or less just bobbing up and down, making the same sort of progress as a cork across a duckpond. Sailing, I was realising, can be a tedious business when in fact there is no sailing to be done. Frustrations creep in : you watch the sky for a hint that the clouds may be getting on the move; you watch the sea for a hint of a wave. And the clouds stay put and the sea stares back at you, and there is just nothing you can do about it. At least, there was nothing *I* could do about it, which was the thing that mattered.

I found myself wondering what I supposed to be doing out

here, anyway – as I had wondered from time to time on the *English Rose* trip. There are two sides to survival – the side you see from the comfort of an armchair at home, when you think how tremendous it would be to pit yourself against the waves; and survival proper, which is what you see when you have made your big effort and got yourself separated from civilization. You are out here, putting up a wonderful feat of endurance – so what? What does it matter? It does not prove a thing. How pointless can you get? What have you done it *for?* It cannot be for enjoyment : you cannot say you enjoy going round the world by yourself in conditions like these unless something has gone adrift among the old grey matter.

I scowled at my meaningless surroundings; made another cup of coffee; marked my chart; made another cup of coffee; scowled a bit more.

I began to talk to myself – not, I should make it clear, because I could not help it, but because I found a quirky pleasure in staging discussions I could not lose. You know :

Blyth : 'That forestay needs tightening. Go and do it.'

Blyth : 'Go to hell.'

Or else :

Blyth : 'That forestay needs tightening. Go and do it.'

Blyth : 'Right you are.'

I also found that doing my sums out loud helped when I was at grips with the mysteries of navigation. And I discovered that as I had not yet swotted up the names of a lot of the bits that went to make up *Dytiscus,* the best thing I could do was to refer to each part by a different number. This was fine, until I forgot which numbers I had given to what.

I read *The Specialist,* a classic of its kind, which Chris and Ruth Waddington had let me have. I found it had a special charm for me, sitting on a bucket in the Bay of Biscay and waiting for the sails to quiver. I always did my bucket-sitting up in the cockpit, weather permitting. Not because of an urge to cling to the land-lubberly tradition which usually requires people to go upstairs for a sit, but because it was just plain pleasant to sit in the sun. At home, you cannot answer nature's call in the sunshine. At least, if you do, you are liable to find that you are telling the chairman of the magistrates all about it and you have your name in the paper the following Friday. So this was a little luxury whose full implications had not crossed my mind when I had agreed to dispense with the toilet: it was a little bonus of unforeseen bliss. I did have an early whirl at bucket-sitting in the saloon, between two upright poles to which I clung devotedly as the boat rose and fell. But I soon found the cockpit more congenial: apart from the sunshine aspect, there was the space factor – less room to fall about and greater opportunity for wedging myself tight while I got on with my reading or checked my charts. It was a bit upsetting one day, though. I was in there giving the old brain a gentle bending as I unhurriedly put the world to rights, when a wave came right over the side and soaked me. It quite took the joy out of it.

Sunday, June 16, brought me my swordfish – a splendid fellow who came quite close, leaping out of the water. I dashed for my camera but I was not quick enough. It was also the day when I worked out a sight which indicated that I had sailed out of my first set of books and charts; and the day for my weekly shave and all-over wash – an old *English Rose* custom which I had never been able to fault in the North Atlantic.

It is really marvellous, the feeling of sluicing the salt from your beard and then of banishing the beard itself. Suddenly, you are clean again. You feel you can take whatever the next seven days have in mind for you. I got out of my sailing gear and into tee-shirt and shorts and I felt seven feet tall. The day called for a celebration. I found myself a tin of Scotch herrings – the first tin I had tackled since I had set out. And then I discovered the snag: no tin-opener. My fault again: Maureen had made a point of asking me at one stage of the packing process if I had got a tin-opener. My reply, snarled with the venom of a hard-pressed citizen who had more important things to think of, had been: 'Of course I've got a tin-opener!' For the rest of the trip, opening a tin was going to mean thumping a screwdriver with a hammer. I had to wedge the tin in a corner so that it could not escape, place one end of my screwdriver on the selected spot of the lid, then clout the other. As a method of effecting an entry, it was not tidy. On the contrary, it was one which prompted the tin to fight back with the only means at its disposal, which invariably involved a jet of juice shooting into the air. The saloon, which was the normal scene of my endeavours, became a place of lingering flavours, from herrings downwards.

Food, naturally, had been a major consideration in my planning. I had budgeted for plenty of it because I had found all I wanted to find about starving at sea when John and I had watched our stocks dwindle remorselessly while we grew weaker every day. But this time I had overbudgeted. I had allowed for four thousand calories a day and I was getting through about two thousand. Better too much than too little – but it would be wonderful to have Maureen and Samantha here to help me with it . . . .

I found it hard to convince myself that there was any good reason why Maureen should not be with me. I was supposed to be racing other people round the world, single-handed, but it would have been hard to find anything less like a race than this. John Ridgway must be about four hundred miles in front of me, and I was to all intents and purposes doing absolutely nothing about catching him up. *Dytiscus* was still bobbing up and down on a windless sea and the sun was smiling at me on my bucket. The thing somehow failed to match – for example – the pace, the pressure and the perspiration which the Oxford and Cambridge lads manage to get into *their* boat race. I looked at Maureen in the galley : she would have been a marvellous crew, and I knew she would have come like a shot if I had asked her. But I could not ask her because, unbelievably, this was supposed to be a race – a single-handed race. Yet already I knew that I did not care about the race; that I would be happy to get round in one piece.

The radio brought bad news on June 18. A French competitor in the solo transatlantic race was in trouble with his catamaran. It was said to be breaking up and there was no sign of him although three aircraft were looking for him. It reminded me forcibly of my responsibilities to myself and to Maureen : you have to know your position the whole of the time. I turned my radio to 2182 mega-cycles, the distress frequency, and I went on bobbing. Next day, there was still no sign of the Frenchman. I wrote in my log : 'I am going to make a bigger effort to pinpoint my position from dead reckoning. I don't feel that this time I am going to die. When the time comes, I will know, and, please God, He will help me to face it – but I don't think it's this trip.'

I realized suddenly that I had lost the cross which Maureen had given me – one which she had had for years. This was bad : I had already lost the St Christopher which she gave me when she kissed me goodbye. Odd, how little things like that can be of discon-certing significance when they are a secret shared only with the ocean.

The complete absence of any wind had by now convinced me

that John and I would have done better if we had waited a month before setting off : a July start, which was what I had originally planned, would surely have yielded the weather we needed. As it was, it was going to take me three weeks to reach Madeira, compared with Sir Francis's eight days. All I was doing was to make unnecessary inroads into my food and water. I decided to ration myself to three pints a day instead of four. The whole thing so far was remarkably similar to the start of the *English Rose* trip : it took John and me about three weeks to get to the Gulf Stream and begin to feel we were making some progress. Again and again, the words which had meant so much to us on *Rosie* kept coming back to me : *Above all, patience.* That was the thing which a well-wisher at Cape Cod had told us we would need. How right she had been. Strengthened, I steeled myelf again to watch the sails, sagging and unmoving. They were like me : totally unemployed.

But June 20 did have a bright spot : the Frenchman had been found in the Atlantic. I wrote my log that night with a suddenly lighter heart. 'What wonderful news. A great boost to my morale. I can just imagine how he feels. Once again, God plays a major role.'

These first two weeks saw me convinced that I could not possibly treat this round-the-world business as a race. There was nothing tangible about it, nothing real; nothing which seemed to have any sense or purpose. Bob up, bob down, bob up, bob down. I was supposed, according to my books and charts, to be able to expect winds for ninety-five per cent of the time, but I reckoned I had had seventy per cent calms. But at least I had got a tan. And I reckoned I had only another four thousand six hundred and eighty miles to go before I had to turn left at the Cape of Good Hope. *Above all, patience.*

I had noticed on the few occasions when the boat had a breeze behind her and was actually making some headway that the trim seemed to be wrong. The new boom which I had had put in seemed to be too heavy, and when the boat rolled the mainsail flapped with a great cracking noise. I realized, naturally, that I had possibly failed to set it properly – but against that was the thought that after two weeks at sea even I ought to have begun to cotton on to the basics. I wondered if the weight distribution was wrong, and I decided to have a bit of a move round. I thought perhaps I needed a bit more weight in the stern.

Sunday, June 23, came and went without my weekly wash. The generator was in the cockpit charging the batteries, and I did not want to run the risk of throwing water onto it and putting it out of action, which could have been a possibility. There was not room for both of us in the cockpit and I could not use it in the saloon because of the fumes.

An eventuality I had not foreseen was brought home to me when I tried to use the remainder of a pint carton of long-life milk on my cornflakes. It had gone sour because it had been opened and left. This meant I could only have milk only once a day until I got out of the sun. Next day, I had my pint in one go – to celebrate throwing away thirty-five days' rations, apart from the goodies like prawn curries and Smarties, to give me a bit more space. Solitary sailors celebrate the oddest things.

Soon I had cause for even more rejoicing. I made radio contact with Madeira and sent a message to Maureen. It went: 'Position 33 degrees 30' North, 17 degrees 20' West. Progress slow. Light winds. Calm. All is well. Missing you both. Any reply. Metrobeale.'

Metrobeale was our code word. It was one which foxed radio operators the whole of the trip, but there was nothing very complicated about it really. It had started one day when I sat down and wrote a list of the things that make up love – then I juggled them about and tried to make a word with their initial letters.

I realised I had achieved another success when a recourse to dead reckoning combined with a sighting of Madeira indicated that I was only four miles out in my calculations. Not bad, I felt, for the novice of the Nab Tower.

And when the sea stirred itself to a big swell, its first exercise on my behalf for days, I really began to think that things were running my way at last. I was like an urchin with the key to the jam cupboard. This time, I celebrated by having half a pint of milk – fresh – on another bowl of cornflakes, and using the other half pint in a drink of hot chocolate.

What is more, I turned the saloon light on for the first time. Until then, I had always used a torch down below after dark, thinking to conserve the batteries by limiting them to the navigation lights and radio. But that night reminded me how pleasant it was to be able to see.   After that, the saloon light went on every night.

After two weeks of having the sea to myself, moreover, I had now begun to see ships. The lights fairly mesmerized me. They made a wonderful end to a day which had suddenly made sense for me. The nothingness had gone. I had sent a message to Maureen, I had beaten my navigation, and the weather was becoming helpful at last. My elation showed signs of getting a bit above itself : I wrote out eight telegrams to various people. Then I looked up the cost in one of the many books with which I was equipped and decided not to send them. But I resolved to try to send another one to Maureen the next day. Meanwhile, it struck me that there was a final job which cried out to be done while I was on the crest of my bubbling wave. So I cleaned my precious plaque – the one which said, 'Oh, God, Thy sea is so great and my boat is so small.' The dorymen of Cape Cod, who used boats like *English Rose* for fishing off Cape Cod and Newfoundland, had fastened it on *English Rose* the day before John and I had left to row home. Now it was fastened on the inside of my cabin door.

The next day worked out splendidly, too, despite initial difficulties in re-establishing radio contact with Madeira after sending my second telegram to Maureen. I could not get a peep out of them and I failed to raise a ship. I felt flat, empty. The wind must have sensed it, because it crept away and left me to my thoughts.

That evening, I tuned in to 2182 after making myself some coffee – and up came Madeira Radio with a call for me. I almost threw myself at it to reply, but I could not get my transmitter to work. Desperately, I changed the mouthpiece and tried again. This time, almost beside myself with panic, I got through. Maureen's message was : 'Telegram received. Ridgway approximately three hundred miles ahead of you. *Opus* lying fourth. All is well. Three of us praying for your safe return. All our love Metrobeale.'

This was a marvellous moment. In a trice, the useless days of bobbing in the Bay of Biscay all seemed worth while. In their own time, they had brought me within reach of home again. I was over the moon with the delirious joy of it all. That was splendid news about Brian Cooke's progress with *Opus* in the solo transatlantic race, too. I could not help feeling that it was rather appropriate that he should have come into the message. After all, this was my finest, maddest moment of the trip so far – and I probably would not have been out here to make the most of it if it had not been for Brian, the man who put me in touch with Ronald Nierop, my sporting sponsor.

As for my own race, I was not to know that Maureen, Frank

Allen and Bill Cottell had decided to tell me that John Ridgway was a hundred miles further in front of me than he actually was. This was a deep-laid plot to spur me to greater efforts, and I was not let into the secret until long after it had all ceased to matter.

I was puzzled, though, about Maureen's mathematics. For the life of me, I could not think who were the three people praying for me. Maureen was one and little Samantha would be Number Two, whether she knew it or not. But who on earth was Number Three? I puzzled for a long time before it struck me.

Colonel – our labrador.

5

First Gale

Chay Blyth : June 26 – July 16

*B*Y now, my days had begun to fall into some sort of routine. I was up at dawn to check the sails and re-set them if necessary, record the log reading, plot my position and wind my watches. My watches, that is to say, and my clocks : I had eleven of them. There were a big eight-day brass clock, a ship's clock, three alarm clocks, one travelling clock, one stopwatch and four wristwatches. Doing my duty by them was quite a performance – ten of them requiring my services every day and the eleventh on Sundays. But then, time was pretty important.

Next, I measured out my daily ration of water and settled to breakfast, which was usually cornflakes, scrambled eggs, and apple flakes or porridge, followed by coffee. After washing up, I spent five minutes cleaning my teeth, then I combed my hair and made my bed – an operation which consisted of folding my sleeping bag and straightening my pillow. That was all there was to it, which helps to explain why I did it every morning.

Then I listened for a time signal and corrected my watches before getting on with chores like finding bits of *Dytiscus* which needed oiling, or swilling down the deck, or tidying the saloon. I had time to read a couple of chapters of whatever book I was on at the moment before taking a noon sight. Then came a chart check, a lunch of cheese and biscuits, and an afternoon nap before settling to write my log, cooking my evening meal, and turning in for the night. The weather, naturally, was always liable to interfere with such orderly arrangements.

A day or two beyond Madeira, the weather did just that. I woke up to a force seven wind, which is between 28 and 33 knots and officially classed as a near-gale, and realized that this was the opportunity for a spot of sails practice. I worked my way down to storm jib and two reefs in the main, found that *Dytiscus* was yawing

because she still had too much canvas, and decided to go one further
and have my first crack at the trysail. I do not know what Neville
would have thought, but this was an operation which took me two-
and-a-half hours to accomplish, instead of the forty minutes which
might be considered a reasonable time by an expert. I had blocks to
fix into place, ropes to get out and uncoil; I had to take down the
mainsail completely, unhook it from the main slide; fit in the trysail
with the realization that I was about two pairs of hands short when
I sought to prevent it flapping during the fitting process; unshackle
the main halyard from the mainsail and fasten it to the trysail;
fix a downhaul to the bottom of the trysail and shackle up the end
of the trysail with two sheets – ropes, to landlubbers! – and finally,
with the object of the exercise hoisted, I had to pull down on the
downhaul and tighten up all round.

The problem with which I was beset was that my knowledge
of the trysail was limited to having seen a photograph of it in
position : I had no idea how it actually got there. After each move,
I had to stand back and think what might reasonably be required
of me next, and then I went uncertainly into action again. I was
scrambling about, falling over myself and generally exuding an
aura of total inefficiency, and I was so preoccupied that when the
wind dropped I did not notice it. Eventually, I stood back to admire
my work – and found that the crew of a ship which I had not until
this moment noticed were lining the rail and pointing at this peculiar
character who was apparently trying to progress with the minimum
of canvas in no wind. I could imagine the skipper saying, 'Hell,
he's not taking any chances.'

As the days passed, the heat was becoming quite a problem.
It was bouncing off the light grey cockpit and dry-frying me. And
down below there was hardly any air because the hatchway had
been sealed in case it was blown off by the wind or blasted off by
a wave, and three of the five air vents had been sealed as well, in
case water came in. It was stifling downstairs and almost totally
unshaded upstirs. I developed my own cooling system : an occasional
bucket of sea water, tipped over the top of my head. And at night
I used fresh water to swill the salt off me. I consoled myself with
the thought that I had known it hotter when I was in Aden, and I
demolished my final fresh orange.

Monday, July 1, was the day which gave me the first idea of
what would be in store for me in the roaring forties. The wind was

about force seven when I got up at 0730 hours, so I took down the No. 1 jib and went under storm jib while I showed an innocent's contempt for the possibilities by going and having my breakfast. Halfway through, it happened: a wave caught us and spun us sideways-on to its roaring advance. Crazily, we bucketed in front of it, the mast threatening to dip almost horizontal. Everything loose on board had developed a life of its own. Charts, books, crockery – they all joined in the new mad game of throwing themselves at each other and at me. The wind hissed like an angry snake in the rigging and a bosomy sea did deep-breathing exercises in a dark satin dress, as if biding its time before smacking us again the full length of our beam. The sails were making their contribution to the pandemonium by whooshing and crackling like mad, threatening to wrench every shackle loose. I grabbed, desperately, and held on to the corner of flailing canvas. Sliding, stumbling, I somehow began to lower the sails as a green Niagara cascaded repeatedly across the deck. I praised my lifeline and went on struggling to subdue the salt-soaked sails which only a day or two earlier had been begging for wind. An eternity later, the sails were down. For the next one-and-three-quarter hours, I lay a-hull, tossing like a cowboy on a rodeo ride and praying for the sea to get tired. I realized how utterly insignificant I was, trapped in the middle of this screaming hell of white-foamed, implacable, raging nature.

Eventually, I decided to risk hoisting the storm jib and get under way.

This was my first gale in a sailing boat, and I was realizing that there is a big difference between facing bad weather in a yacht and facing it in an open rowing boat. A rowing boat will go up and down with the waves, and as long as you can bale out the water more or less quickly as it comes in there is no damage done. With a yacht, however, the wind has something to go at. Things can come loose on the deck and begin flying about with every prospect of causing considerable damage. A rampant boom, for example, is no mean adversary on a switchback sea.

This was also my first chance to appreciate – if that is the word I want – the full implications of the doubts which my advisers had been expressing about the yacht's ability to run before the wind. The waves curled round it, lifting the stern, and *Dytiscus* simply turned sideways-on: 'broached', if I may try one of my new-found sailing terms on you. These were conditions with which the self-steering gear had never been intended to cope. So I lowered the sails again, and once I had lowered them there was nothing more I could do except pray. So I prayed. And between times I turned to one of my sailing manuals to see what advice it contained for me : it was like being in hell with instructions. I was lonely and I was frightened. And I realized that this was but a foretaste of what was going to come once I reached the Roaring Forties in my strong but totally unsuitable boat.

I was not blaming the boat, and I am still not doing so. Now that it is all over, I realize more than ever that if Westfield Engineering had not made it the solid job that it is, it is unlikely that I would have been in a position to try to swing my sorrows on to *Dytiscus* even if I had wanted to. The punishment which the boat took was totally unrelated to the purpose for which it had been constructed. Certainly, the boat made life difficult. But, beyond all doubt, it was the boat that kept life possible.

The fact that *Dytiscus* survived where it had never been intended to survive also made me realize that a Providence beyond man's comprehension was looking after me. In my log that night, I wrote : 'It has died down a bit now, after I had prayed for it to go down. Nobody on this earth could convince me that there is no Lord. I call it a Third Force, but it's the same. This is the best place in the world for character-forming, no matter who you are. Anybody out here on his own soon swallows humble pie.'

Next day, after a night in which I was up and down from my bunk like a yo-yo, the hammering continued. Grey-green mountains would pick the boat up by its over-buoyant stern and *Dytiscus* would go into her helpless crab act, and the self-steering gear would not bring her round again. I could not help feeling depressed when I began reading Sir Francis Chichester's book again and compared the equipment he had with mine. I tried to console myself by thinking that my troubles might be entirely due to me, and that if this were so there was a chance that I might have improved my techniques by the time I was really going to need them, down in the forties. There just had to be a solution. It was up to me to find it.

Meanwhile, I was speeding southwards, and just slightly to the west, at between four and five knots. The gale was at least blowing the right way! I found a dead flying fish on the deck, a silver-blue fellow victim of the storm. It was a sight which somehow made me very sad.

I wondered how John Ridgway was. I had a feeling that the loneliness which was gnawing at me was probably leaving him untroubled – and that thought made me envious. My sense of being on my own was not helped by my failure to make contact with the Cape Verde Islands, about five hundred miles west of Dakar. I wanted to send a telegram to ask Charlie Brooker about the eyebolts at the foot of the mast, which I suspected of being brass. If they were, I feared that some sort of reaction – electrolysis – would start between them and the aluminium of the mast itself. I was to find later that there was no such possibility, and I should never even have suspected it, because Charlie had gone over the mast with unhurried competence.

I also wanted to let Maureen know where I was. Every time I thought of her – which was most of the time – I could picture her, worried into knots about me but not letting anybody suspect. You cannot teach her anything about inner toughness. Lord, she needed every scrap of it, the way I was taking advantage of it.

The weather was still fairly dirty, and I could not risk putting the generator into the cockpit to charge the batteries, in case water got into it. I could not use it in the cabin because of the fumes. And if I did not charge the batteries, my hopes of raising Cape Verde on my radio were that much less.

My efforts to sew the storm jib clew – that is the corner to which are fastened shackles and sheets for extending and securing it – reinforced my faith that somebody was looking after me. I broke the needle, which I knew was the only one of that size I had with me. But when I started sorting out my sail repair kit I found an identical needle which should never have been there – hidden in a roll of whipping twine. My delight was distracted when I tipped a mug of hot coffee over and burned my foot. This was a minor disaster I could have done without. I was already a bit concerned about my hands, which were scaling and flaking because of the salt spray, and I did not really want to have to start thinking about my foot as well.

My navigation was showing no sign of giving me anything to tell my grandchildren about. My dead reckoning put me smack in the middle of the Ila de St Antao and my sight agreed with it. The problem was that I could not see St Vincente, and I was a bit aware that this ought to make me an optician's nightmare: St Vincente is five thousand nine hundred and seventy-one feet high.

Admittedly, the visibility was not all that good, but even so I felt that if I really was within spitting distance of a pimple as prominent as that one, then I should be able to spot it. I kept jumping up and down, to extend my desperate horizon by the vital fraction that might make all the difference. It didn't. No pimple, no spots. Was my log not working properly? Was my astro completely wrong? I just went on heading south, and I found the whole thing totally unnerving. What the hell was the matter? And when I heard on my radio that Alec Rose, the first yachtsman to follow Sir Francis, had just crossed the finishing line in *Lively Lady,* my spirits really plummetted. God, how I wished that I was there, too.

And yet, and yet . . . .

Once again, just as I was in need of a morale-booster, I got one. I made contact with the *Marco R,* a Liberian tanker berthed at Mindello, in the Cape Verde Islands. The radio operator, Richard Pollard, turned out to be a most helpful character. He took two messages for me – one to send birthday wishes to Samantha for July 19 and to ask Maureen to check on the metal which was used for the downhaul eyebolts at the mast base; and the other to my old schoolfriend, Frank Scott, up in Hawick, asking him to give Maureen all the help he could with the cottage.

Richard Pollard said I was lucky because he had picked me up after switching to 2182 kcs, which was something he rarely did. It may have seemed just luck : I knew better.

I ended my message to Maureen : 'Next Cape Town, if contact can be made. Reply Mindello Radio. Metrobeale.'

Like every other radio operator, Richard Pollard was intrigued by Metrobeale, the word I had made as I sat in a snowhouse in Canada in January, 1963, when the wind was howling outside and the temperature was thirty degrees below freezing. It was the word which had stayed with me as a permanent link with the Arctic survival course which had been the Army's reason for putting me there.

My radio also brought me Alec Rose's reception. I heard him say his experiences had made him feel very humble, and I knew exactly what he meant. But it was wonderful to be able to listen to him, just as if I were sitting at home in Portsmouth. Then they played Louis Armstrong's 'What a Wonderful World' and I looked at Maureen and Samantha and I blinked back an insistent tear. More than ever, I was determined I was not going to die on this trip.

What I wrote as I rolled with my angry sea was :

'I want to live and enjoy being with my wife and child. If I don't think this boat will take it, then I will put into port and fly home. I feel the Lord is with me. He has helped me a terrific amount already and I pray He will watch over us all the time that is in front of us.'

The calm came again on Friday, July 5, when I was about twelve miles west of the most westerly outpost of the Cape Verde Islands, which I could see climbing hazily out of the sea. The self-steering gear must have been glad to have the pressure eased. A check during the night had revealed that two nuts were missing and four screws were loose. I did my repairs in the dark and thanked God that nothing more drastic had happened.

It was a day for *Dytiscus* to bob and for me to do odd jobs like making a couple of warps. And it ended with an evening shared with a bright silver moon and a flat and twinkling sea. There was not a breath of wind. I sat on the deck with my mug of coffee, looking at the heavens and listening to my radio playing quiet music which seemed to have been picked for this very scene. As usual, I thought of home. As I thought, I found myself a new target : if I could be near Cape Town by September 29, I would be able to send Maureen birthday wishes. As usual, I had the date wrong : every year, I have to be told it is September 26.

Days passed, and so at last did the Cape Verde Islands. At one time, I had begun to think I was doomed to look at them for the rest of my life, because *Dytiscus* bobbed on unabatedly and progress was just about imperceptible. I was getting nowhere, and I did not even have the consolation that I was getting nowhere fast. I cheered up with every puff of wind, but when my sails sagged I sagged with them.

Whenever there was the slightest breeze, flying fish seemed determined to keep me company. One night, I threw nine of them back after they had landed on the deck. I would be lying on my bunk and there would be a sudden, gentle thump from above, followed by a frantic scuttering sound as my visitor tried to frighten death away. I would dash upstairs to the rescue. Nine times is a lot of times : several times, I said that I would not bother again – but then I told myself that it did not seem much of an effort to make to save a life. I could have eaten the poor little devils, like other solo sailors do, but I had made my own private bargain with the fish : I would not eat them if they would not eat me.

But if the sound of flying fish was a sound that came with a breeze, there were other, quite different sounds which I learned were the sounds of a boat which chafes at enforced inactivity in a calm. The rigging sways gently with the swell and the sail makes helpless gestures as the boom moves, too. *Flup . . . flup . . . flup.* You despair of a breeze, and you lower your sail, and you get the *ksssht* of the ropes and halyards against the mast. There is the slupping of a disinterested sea against the hull; the chockling *cloink* of tins of provisions edging against each other down below.

These are the sounds that make thinking easy. Life, you discover you are profoundly aware, is not the materialistic business it was before you sailed away from it. It is about giving your children a moral and a spiritual leg-up, so that they will turn out better than you have. It is the pleasure of doing all you can for those about you. The pity, I told myself one day when I had caught myself going firmly philosophical, is that you have to get yourself into a pointless situation like this one before it dawns on you.

Monday, July 8, did not give me much time for thinking. The sun turned out in force, the breeze came back from its holiday, and *Dytiscus* fairly skipped along. The only problem was that to make the best use of the wind I had to edge east all the time and I had almost reached the 25° West mark again. My hope was to stay between 25° and 27° West, although Sir Francis went as far as 23° West. My ambitions had to be limited because *Dytiscus* could not sail as close to the wind as *Gipsy Moth* could.

Apart, however, from this slight concern about my direction, I had a glorious day. I changed course no fewer than nine times to keep up the pace, working like a beaver all day in my sailing cap and sunglasses. But I did dress for dinner. That is to say, I donned a teashirt – and a pair of trousers. And dinner that night tasted particularly good : this had been the best day's sailing since I had started. It was acknowledged in my despatch of the last of my potatoes, boiled with rice and topped with margarine, and accompanied by reconstituted prawns and my final onion. It was only as I was working my way through the meal that it occurred to me that I had had rice every day since June 8.

A noon sight next day put me at 11° 45′ North, which should have meant the end of the North-East Trade Winds. The Doldrums would be next; back on my course of south-west, I hoped that some miracle would push me through them with a minimum of bobbing. I felt I had done my fair share of bobbing already.

By this time, the BBC's World Service was fading, and I would soon have to hunt for a new channel. But it managed to give me a splendid surprise by coming up with a recording of Matt Monroe singing 'Born Free' – played for John Ridgway at the request of his wife, Marie-Christine, for the first birthday of their daughter, Rebecca Louise. *Keep going, John: I'm not far behind you!*

I had some more companions for fifteen minutes when a score of dolphins began to take an interest in me. They kept cutting across the bow, as if to see how close they could come, like a bunch of blue-chinned urchins playing 'last across' in a busy street. I took some photographs then hunted out my cine camera, which agreed to work only spasmodically, even after I had thumped it into calling off a complete withdrawal of labour.

I lunched magnificently on corn beef, cheese, coffee, honey and biscuits. The corn beef was the important part : I had opened the tin because I needed it as a do-it-yourself repair kit for the self-steering gear. The servo blade was being worn by the adjusting screw, and I thought a tin shield would improve matters. Somehow or other, I never got round to using it and finding out. A bit of improvization which did come in handy enabled me to top up my water supply with twelve gallons when the rains came : I hung a bucket over the forward end of the boom, pausing only to thank heaven that I had brought two of them.

By keeping the mainsail up, I could collect the rain and watch it run down the boom and into the bucket.

Slowly, the days passed. I made perhaps ninety miles in forty-eight hours, which was slow, slow going. I made friends with my dolphins on their return by throwing them Smarties. I leaned over the side to watch them and discovered I was collecting barnacles. I admired a shoal of fleeting mauve-coloured fish. I studied the onset of rust. And I cracked my barometer glass by thumping it with my spare wind vane as I was re-arranging some equipment in the saloon.

I found by trial and error that the nearest I could sail to the south-west wind was only about sixty degrees, instead of the comfortable forty degrees which a racing boat can normally manage. If I went too close, the self-steering gear would cause *Dytiscus* to yaw quite violently. And under trysail and storm jib I could get only ninety degrees to the wind. One day, I covered ninety-eight miles, but finished up only sixty-five miles further south than I had been at daybreak. Admittedly, I wanted to get some way to the east, ready for being pushed west with the current and the South-East Trades – but what I wanted above all was to get south.

At the same time, every mile south was a mile nearer both the Equator and the Roaring Forties, and I would not say I was over-keen at either porspect. The Equator was bothering me because I had visions of running into even more trouble with my navigation than I had found already. So far, I had been doing my sums with varying degrees of success, but south of the Equator I would have to get to grips with a different set of sums and the thought was something which I, as a quite astonishingly non-mathematical man, found distinctly alarming.

As for the Roaring Forties, I was reading Sir Francis's account of the waves and the weather in those parts and I felt no compulsion whatever to get there and check up on him. Two other problems were my inability for some reason to get any time signals, which are vital for navigation ; and my steady progress towards the east, which was threatening to take me further in that direction than I wanted to go.

I tried to cheer up with a tin of sardines. I failed, but trying was very pleasant : sardines ranked as goodies, for limited use only. As a matter of fact, I was by this time eating very little, because it was eighty-one degrees in the cabin, with its sealed hatchway – hardly the sort of condition for inducing healthy vitamin-mangling in a novice who was beginning to wonder just what he had bitten off in deciding to pit his ignorance against the ocean.

The boat shuddered as a wave took it unawares. And I knew there would be plenty more shudders in the weeks to come.

6

Disaster and Diversions

Chay Blyth : July 17 – August 15

WITH the winds just east of south and striking force six or
seven, I began making good progress towards the Equator.
I made my position 2° 33′ North, and I wanted to cross the
line inside forty-eight hours so that it could happen on Samantha's
first birthday. It was not going to be the sort of birthday present
she would think much of, but it was going to do me the world
of good – even if I did not know what I was letting myself in for
on the other side. This round-the-world business was called a race,
but the only person I could compete with was me. For all practical
purposes, nobody else existed. You cannot think of it as a race
when you can look in all directions and see quite clearly that you
have the ocean to yourslf. In circumstances like these, the whole
exercise assumes an air of unreality. You can crash ahead and ask
yourself why you are bothering, or you can bob becalmed with the
feeling that you are not really losing ground, because there is so
plainly nobody to lose ground to.

Just now, I was nothing like becalmed. The boat was vibrating
more and more often as the winds and the waves stepped up their
attentions, and I was receiving an insight into the cocktail's end of
cocktail-shaking. I had a shock when I went into the forward compartment for a bag of rations : the place was awash. Because I was
going to windward, the water had begun to pour through the two
vents which I had left unsealed. They were unsealed because somebody had said that water never came in there, and because I had
been in no position to know otherwise. There was more to come :
I discovered that the double-action pump in the port locker, from
which I had removed the toilet, was also leaking. Because we were
heeling over at an angle of thirty degrees, the pump was lower
than the outlet – and water was coming down the outlet, filling the
pump and pouring over my two-pound box of caramels. I had to

71

throw the lot away. The saloon carpet was sodden and water was sloshing about beneath the leeward bunk. I mopped up as best I could, then stuffed the vents with cloths and sealed the pump outlet. For good measure, I put a polythene box beneath the pump.

As if to prevent my feeling under-occupied, my speedometer stopped functioning. It had never been particularly precise either about distance or speed, but at least it gave me something to work on when I tried to decide what sort of progress I was making, and I did not relish the idea of pressing on without it. I had by now acclimatized to the system : if it told me I was doing ten knots, I knew I was doing seven. But, suddenly it was telling me nothing – and to reach its working parts I had to unload the whole of the rope locker, which resembled a general stores that someone had tried to push over.

Apart from the ropes and sea anchors, there were five bags of rations, each weighing ten pounds, and several boxes of eggs, plus four five-gallon jerrycans which each weighed fifty pounds. And it was not just a question of heaving them about and dumping them on the floor, because the floor was sloping at a thirty-degree angle and would have been inclined to discourage anything to stay where I put it, even if *Dytiscus* had not been jumping like beads on a belly dancer. Somehow, I eventually burrowed through to the speedo's handle, which was set into the hull. I unscrewed it, and by dint of some frantic fingerwork I replaced it with a blanking cap before I had shipped too much of the Mid-Atlantic – but it was a desperate moment. It is not exactly an inspiring sight when water comes rushing into a boat even when you are sitting in harbour. When you know that it is three miles to the sea-bed, the whole thing somehow fails to have you baying for more. However, I managed to repair it and escaped with nothing more serious than a pair of wet knees when I removed the blanking cap to replace it. Then I did my re-packing among the distractions of *Dytiscus*'s dervish dance. From start to finish, the operation took ninety minutes – and I did not break a single egg. And people wonder why Britain is Great.

I had my award for good conduct sooner than I expected. Out of curiosity, I tried for a time signal – and got one, my first for several days. There are stations at strategic points round the world which provide a time signal service on five, ten, fifteen or twenty-five megacycles. Mine came through, very faintly, on fifteen. Time, as I have said, is very important to a sailor, and even more important to a novice like me. Every second out in your time means a mile out in calculating your position.

My sundry preoccupations rather threw my routine out of gear. Breakfast took the form of porridge and coffee at 1400 hours after a noon sight. Fighting the thirty-degree list, I took a wander with my coffee and noticed that the blue ink from the plastic food bags had been encouraged to make its mark over a wide radius because of all the water which had found its way aboard. And I managed to get a splinter in my foot, which gave me my first chance to operate on myself. Perhaps it did not match up to the marvels of do-it-yourself dentistry, which I hoped I would not have to tackle, but at least it was something. With my magnifying glass and needle, I felt like a cross between Sherlock Holmes and Dr Kildare.

The Equator came the next day, July 18, at 2134 hours, which was just under two-and-a-half hours too soon for my hopes to be there on Samantha's birthday. The wind had begun to come from the south-east, which made me think I had found the Trades at last. I hoisted the No. 1 jib and pressed on at about six knots, sailing comfortably. I could have used more canvas, but that would have given the self-steering gear too much to cope with. I was in no hurry. I knew that John was probably crashing ahead as fast as he could go, but I did not want to risk anything which would force me to have to put in to port. I had a feeling that if I did put in, I would not want to set off again – because I would know the conditions which were waiting for me, and I would quite rightly feel that I had too much to lose. If I could, I wanted to get round non-stop. Survival, rather than speed, was the thing.

Survival meant Maureen and Samantha : – little Sammy, twelve months old on Friday, July 19. And wonderful, wonderful Maureen.

I celebrated the birthday by deciding not to do anything about the saloon carpet, which I found was wet again as soon as I got up at 0745 hours. This was to be no day for work. I had a birthday breakfast of grapefruit juice, scrambled eggs, coffee and biscuits; and a birthday shave followed by handfuls of after-shave. I made my bed, tidied up, and dug out Samantha's birthday pack – the first of Maureen's special parcels. I was hoping to find a note inside, because she always manages to squeeze a note in somewhere when I go off on some adventure

Out of the pack came some baby gift-wrap paper containing a

cake which had been baked by Betty Ridley. There was a tin holding
one candle to go with it. Next came a bar of Highland Toffee, a
tin of chicken, a tin of pâté, a tin of rice. And a tartan-wrapped
parcel labelled 'To be opened when bored.' I was so excited that I
simply had to declare myself bored. It contained a pocket solitaire
and a book of crossword puzzles. But there was no note. My spirits
dropped. This was disastrous.

I propped the big photograph up by my bed; said a little prayer;
had a little cry. I knew that some time today Maureen would cry,
too – probably when she gave Samantha the gold bracelet which I
bought for her birthday before I left. A Dewar's whisky cheered
me up a bit. I toasted Samantha's birthday, Maureen, myself, and
the future. It was time to play some taped music. I put on one that
I picked at random and settled to listen. Halfway through, I sat up
as if spiked with a bradawl : there was Maureen, with a message
for me.

This was unbelievable. I found later that this was the only tape
on which she had spoken – and I could have chosen to play any one
of the other fourteen which I had on board. Maureen had asked me
if I would like her to record a message, and I had said I would not
because I thought it would upset me. She had nevertheless slipped
this one in, and I had found it on Samantha's birthday in spite of
the odds against my doing so. Coincidence? I did not think so –
not for a moment. I said a little prayer of thanks before taking a
noon sight.

This showed that I had covered a hundred and twenty miles in
twenty-four hours. I did not think that was bad, considering that
I had three hundred and twenty square feet of sail all told. Sir
Francis had had six hundred square feet in his big genoa alone.
As this was my first day in the Southern Hemisphere, I took another
sight later. I wanted to make sure I was managing the navigation
change-over. I was. My gratitude went out, not for the first time,
to Neville Wood.

Despite my pre-breakfast intentions of having an easy day, I
spent most of the afternoon scooping water from beneath the false
floor of the saloon. I removed nearly two gallons, which left another
three still there. Then I had dinner. Grapefruit juice; pâté; chicken,
tinned celery, creamed potatoes with plenty of margarine; creamed
rice – I was still not tired of rice; cheese and biscuits; coffee. I lit
the candle on Samantha's cake and took a couple of photographs;

blew it out and cut the cake. With Maureen's message playing, I toasted Mum and daughter.

The sound of Maureen's voice was tying me in knots. I still could not believe that this was really happening – that I was really listening to the wonderful girl who, for the second time in our short marriage, had put everything she could into backing me in a crazy adventure. The words came simple and direct, straight from her heart, the way they always do with Maureen. I pictured her as she spoke them : she must have been in the bedroom, probably sitting on the bed, surrounded by the clutter which had taken charge of our home during those anxious weeks when our preparations were coming to a head. She knew I had said I did not want any messages because I thought they would upset me – but she, bless her heart, had known better. What, after all, is a lump in the throat in exchange for the sheer wonder of an experience like the one which was now mine? Over and over again, I played the message which I was already beginning to know by heart. I picked up the photograph and looked again into those smiling eyes, sparkling symbols of the love and trust and loyalty embodied in the words to which I was listening. *Keep smiling, darling: I'll be back. Here's to you and little Samantha. Happy birthday, Samantha. Just you look after Mummy for me until I come home.*

Then I ate my piece of cake and drank another toast – 'to Absent Friends', to all those who had played a part in getting me on my way. This was a birthday party I would never forget. It was a party whose last two hours I spent lying on the saloon roof with nothing above me but the stars in a clear sky, while the tape recorder played *The Sound of Music* and *My Fair Lady*. I heard my front door bell ringing, and Samantha squealing, and Colonel barking.

It all fitted in with the mood which had been set by Maureen's message ; a mood of glowing nostalgia and gratitude to the girl who had worked so hard in so many ways to make The Big Trip possible.

This was a memorable interlude among hard-working days of squalls and calms, of leaks and mopping up. The water kept gathering beneath the saloon floor and when I went into the forward compartment I found I had a leak there, too, dripping almost fast enough through a join in the roof to be described as running. I did not persuade it to give up trying. For what seemed to be the pushed synthetic rubber all round it, which slowed it down but

umpteenth time, I lifted the saloon carpet. This time, I decided
it was to stay lifted until conditions improved. Meanwhile, things
looked very bare without it. There was not a lot of water there,
and if I had had a bilge into which to pump it a few strokes would
have dealt with it. As it was, however, it was all a matter of faith
and floorcloths, and of trying to get rid of about four gallons a
day the hard way. And I found another leak – in one of the extra
shroud plates which were put in on the starboard side to give
greater strength. Again, I got busy with the synthetic rubber. It was
the same again up forward in the anchor compartment, where the
bulk of the water was coming from. The rubber has to be dry
when you use it, which was a bit problematical in the circumstances.
Out loud, unthinking, I said : 'Oh, for a calm for an hour!' Twenty
minutes later, after days of waves swallowing the boat from bow
to stern – and me as well, if I happened to be in the cockpit –
we had calm for thirty minutes. It was just long enough for the
job I had to do. I looked at the sky and I said thank you to the
Power who was listening to me.

Then we were back to the rough stuff, with grey water spewing
across the saloon roof and the boat jiggling like a tambourine on
overtime. When it got too bad and too wet, I remembered *Rosie*
and told myself I had seen it worse and seen it wetter, and that as
long as the mast stayed up we were in with a chance.

Disaster came on Tuesday, July 23, when I was about seven
hundred and fifty miles west of Ascension Island. The sun came
out and I decided it was time to charge the batteries while there was
a chance. I got out the generator, which was wedged at the end of
the spare bunk in the saloon, and hand-pumped it full of petrol
after connecting it to the extraction point beneath the bunk. Too
late, I realized that the petrol was a sickly white. I feared the worst
and I was right. The generator ran for about two minutes, then
it stopped. I put some petrol on to a piece of paper and tried to
light it. No go. Salt water had found its way into the starboard
bilge keel, where thirty gallons of petrol were stored, just as it had
found its way everywhere else.

What had happened was that water had got into the breather
tube which led into the starboard keel. It had not been difficult for it,
because with the boat to wndward and heeling over on its side the
waves could splash consistently over the tube, which passed inside
one of the deck stanchions and into the hull.

And now, just forty-five days out to sea, my entire stock of petrol was ruined.

No petrol meant no generating. No generating meant no charging the batteries. And when the batteries died, I would not be able to use my radio either to transmit or to receive. Time signals would be out, and if I wanted the 2182 distress frequency I would not be able to get it. I could have no lights, which meant that any ship on collision course with me would simply stay there and be none the wiser. If this happened while I was asleep, *Dytiscus* might achieve a confrontation with a tanker. Try as I might, I could not bring myself to fancy the prospect of crashing through the night with no lights.

But it was the radio business which really bothered me. My wife would neither know where I was nor how I was, and if I decided to stick it out it would be another eight months at least before she would know that I was alive.

I was headed for the Roaring Forties and would have to pass South Africa. When I reached there, I would have my opportunity to obtain replacement petrol and put myself into touch with the world again. To do so, however, would disqualify me from the race in which – entry form or no – I was considered to be competing : the rules were insistent that I should neither touch land nor receive help. But morally, had I the right to let my wife wait eight months, with people constantly asking if she had heard anything, just to satisfy my ego? I was not really interested in somebody sitting behind a desk in London and saying 'You are disqualified.' A wife with faith enough in me to let me go on a crazy venture in the wrong type of boat, totally inexperienced, and with every possibility – as it now appeared – of tackling the Roaring Forties at the worst time of the year, deserved something from me in return.

There was no need for me to make my decision yet : time enough as I approached the Cape, which was still about two thousand five hundred miles away even if I could imitate the no-nonsense attitude of any well-instructed crow. But since six weeks of sailing had given me broken doors, leaks, torn sails and watered petrol, and I had more than that many months – including the really difficult bits – still in front of me, I had some pretty substantial evidence to consider. And it all pointed the same way.

I did, of course, have twenty-four gallons of paraffin on board – in the other bilge keel – for cooking in the event of the calor gas running out, and for emergency heating and lighting. I could convert some of those gallons to lighting purposes, using them with my emergency reserve of hurricane lamps, and risk cold meals in the final stages. Each gallon would give me eight nights of light.

But before I did anything, the sensible precaution was to empty a few containers and transfer my paraffin stock into them, in case water got at that as well. I set about doing so, with a heart that felt heavy enough to sink me without trace.

* * * * * *

The very next day gave despondency another push, despite the inevitable uplift of a bath, shave and hair-wash. I found that my Walker's log was not registering, and when I hauled it inboard the reason was painfully plain : the spinner had gone. It was quite possible that the cause of its disappearance was a peckish shark, but I could hardly believe that so much could have gone wrong in the first four thousand miles of a thirty-thousand-mile journey.

Twenty-four hours later, I found more trouble still. For a change, there was hardly a breath of wind when I awoke, which meant that it was obviously a day for maintenance. And maintenance this time meant trying to mend the leak in the forward compartment, which normally housed the anchor and was intended to be self-draining. There was no anchor in there this trip, however. Our preparations had included filling it with a foam like expanded polystyrene, which hardened off to form a bulkhead for beating off icebergs, or at least giving them something to think about before they ploughed through the rest of the boat. We had screwed the cover down and then sealed the drain hole with a wooden plug. But I now suspected that the water which I had found myself consistently required to mop up in the saloon had found its way through from the forward compartment. And if water was in the forward compartment, it had to be got out. The removal of the cover showed that there was in fact quite a lot of water there. The outlet had obviously to be unbunged. I spent two-and-a-half hours digging a drain channel to the plug through the foam – hacking away about a third of the foam in the process. The plug itself was still inaccessible, however : in spite of my excavations, I could not manoeuvre the drill sufficiently in the cramped space. The only way to get at the plug was from the outside. As it was three inches above the water-line and about three feet below the deck, the operation could hardly help becoming one of the highlights of the trip.

With my lifeline anchored firmly to a strongpoint on the deck, and my feet wedged between two stanchions, I hung upside down above the water and began to attack the plug with a quarter-inch drill. As I was unable to use my hands to hold on to the boat, every increase of pressure on my drill simply caused me to swing away from the hull. The sea joined in the fun by arranging for the occasional wave to immerse me from head to waist and provide intermitten mouthfuls of salt water. I was there for two-and-a-half hours, lost one drill, broke two more, and emerged steeped in admiration for Tony *(Trapeze)* Curtis. The more so, as I knew that by the time he had finished a comparable operation, he would have finished it successfully. I didn't. I got the bung out all right. But it was not long before I was again in full swing with my floorcloth. I never did find out where the water was coming from . . . .

The following day found me doing another conscientious Curtis – this time, up the mast, to overhaul the standing rigging. For a start, I am the wrong shape for shinning up masts. I managed to climb as far as the cross-trees, three-quarters of the way up and twenty-five feet above the deck, but once there I was in trouble. The boat had not stopped rolling for the occasion, and every time it rolled I rolled with it, only more so. I was the end of an outsize pendulum – the end which had to travel an alarming distance to keep up with quite a small movement at the pivotal point on deck. As I swayed backwards and forwards, I clung like a particularly devoted barnacle, unhappily aware that anyone who happened to see me would assume that I was something left over from last season's pantomime. I was festooned like a Christmas tree, with pliers and spanners hanging from my belt and ready for use if ever I could see my way to sparing a hand with which to use them. I couldn't.

I climbed down and tried again, this time with a nylon ladder, which I unsuspectingly began to treat as if it were something good and solid purloined from the fire brigade. I was a mere five rungs up when I found that you do not climb nylon ladders as if they are wooden ones – but that if you do, they stretch and sway, taking you well clear of the comparative safety of the mast, against which you thought you had stretched it tight. So I taught myself to climb the nautical way, of necessity and on the instant, twisting the ladder through my legs to keep it taut as I went. But I was still far from happy. It sounds ridiculous in retrospect, but once I was at the top and looking down, the boat looked so small that I could believe it was possible for me to fall down and miss it. It was all a far cry from the day I had been winched to the top on a mud mooring at Wicor Marine in order that I could see what was up there. Now, in Mid-Atlantic, I played pendulums for perhaps four minutes, pliering here and spannering there and seeking support and reassurance from the shrouds. I vowed I would never play pendulums again – and I only ever did play once more.

One of the insurances I took out to avoid the necessity of going aloft in future was to fix a rope between a cleat and the halyard, which is the rope for raising and lowering the sails. This meant that if the halyard snapped I would not have to monkey upwards in search of the broken end, which would normally have shot up the mast as the sail fell down. I had no idea if this was accepted sailing practice, but it seemed a good idea at the time.

One of my less important odd jobs was to put a few necessary stitches into the jungle bush-hat which had become my sailing cap despite my having invested in the real thing when I first presented myself to Neville Wood.

These and other diversions did not manage to take my mind off the thing which had become the dominant factor of the entire exercise. Now that I could not rely on there being much in the batteries for distress purposes, I had had to do some re-thinking about my course. I had intended to go much further south than Sir Francis did, because it was a shorter route. But if I were to have a chance of getting my weak signal heard it would now be necessary to keep north and do a tighter circle round the Cape of Good Hope.

I had also decided that it was far too early for me to begin using my emergency lighting system, and I did not dare to use what little power was left in the batteries for navigation or other lights. It was very eerie, crashing through the night unilluminated. I adopted a caveman's approach to life: when darkness fell, I went to bed. Bed was a good place to be, in any case, because the weather was becoming distinctly colder, the generator had begun to rust, and I was prey to all my old uncertainties about where I had got to. A great, empty loneliness settled on me. No ships, no sharks, no whales, no dolphins, no porpoises. There was not even any rubbish floating by to cheer me up. This was totally unlike the *English Rose* journey, which produced just about every external distraction imaginable. This time, even the bird life was limited to a solitary albatross – and he abandoned me after spurning some biscuits I threw him.

I was aware of a mental slowing-up. Working out sights had never actually been my most successful way of passing the idle hour. Sometimes they worked, sometimes they did not. But now I had reached the stage where the job was taking much longer.

I found I had to speak my calculations before they would register with me, and I could rely on nothing that I had not checked at least twice. Fiercely, I would say: 'Six and seven. What the dickens is six and seven? *For God's sake, what's six and seven?'* I would then find out by using my fingers. On my good days, of course, there was no problem: 'Six and seven? Nine!'

By July 31, the south-east winds had moved me further west than I would have liked. I had passed the island of Martin Vaz and was 23° 10′ South and 28° 20′ West, so I was thinking hard of the Roaring Forties. My apprehension was based on the fact that I had already broached once. Worse, I knew, was to come. I decided I would head south-east, for Tristan da Cunha, one thousand two hundred miles away, so that I could send a letter to Maureen. It would also be a reliable navigation check for me. So, after eleven days on the starboard tack, August 1 found me heralding a force three wind from the south-west as an indication that I had at last emerged from the South-East Trades. I 'turned left' and got on to the port tack. I wondered if my changed course would find me any new leaks: by this time I had dried and re-laid the carpet.

Progress was slow. For the first few days, it was sixty miles a day, which was half what I hoped for. The winds were negligible. I dug out my Army parachute smock, which still had my wings and my Canadian wings on it, and I began to wear it because each day was becoming colder. That jacket took me back a year or two – to March, 1963, which was the year when John and I had won the Para-chute Brigade Canoe Race after seventy-eight miles of sweat from Reading to Westminster. *John, where are you at this moment?*

Without being too certain about where I was either, I had the feeling that I was going to be there more or less for ever. *Where the hell's that wind?*

I opened two of my boredom parcels. A pack of playing cards, dominoes, miniature ludo, chess. And another box of Highland Toffee. *Bless you, Maureen.* I put up the white heather from the tartan wrapping in the saloon, beside the window. My parachute scarf was there as well, and a row of Maureen's Paisley pattern handkerchiefs beneath. Two blue and two yellow ribbons were brightening up the ceiling : I had flown one off each backstay on leaving the Hamble because my departure had coincided with the Common Riding Festival period in Hawick, when everyone traditionally wears blue and yellow.

Boredom had its marching orders when, in successive days, I burned my right wrist badly while preparing rice in the pressure cooker, found that the starboard locker had sprung a leak, and realized that the rudder had developed a tendency to rise an inch-and-a-half, which was affecting the self-steering gear – and which, in turn, had caused me to stay at the helm one entire night. I decided that the mainsail had begun lifting the rudder because a pin had sheared or a nut had come undone. I rigged a jury line to take the strain and reduced speed to ease the pressure more. I tried not to contemplate the possibility of the rudder's being lifted out altogether and sinking.

There was only one way for me to find out what was the matter. I waited two days for a spot of calm, dropped the sails, climbed into my skin-diving gear, fixed myself up with a snorkel, a knife and two safety lines, and then climbed overboard, feeling doubly umbilical and deeply depressed. I was by this time in blue shark territory, and it was much more likely that my attempts to fix things would attract a shark than an A.A. patrolman.

It was an eerie sensation beneath the surface. The water was as clear as a swimming pool, but this was a pool that was a mile or so deep. I was impressed by *Dytiscus*'s collection of barnacles and I went back for my camera. But I could find nothing wrong with the rudder. The bolts were all in place. I was mystified, but relieved. I broke the surface like a rubber-rigged Aphrodite, climbed back on board and treated myself to a bath.

The wind rose steadily all that afternoon, and the sea swelled self-importantly into a menacing, implacable landscape of marching mountains beneath scudding grey-black clouds. There was a brooding gloom spelling imminent disaster for anything misguided enough to be in the way. Sure enough, when the moment came for me to be put in my place, and the wave entrusted with the duty rose to collect me, *Dytiscus* did not hestitate : we broached. Sideways to the sea, we took a battering the length of the beam as a storm of green rain swept over us.

The self-steering gear tried to right us, but the force of the gale against the vane caused the vane clutch to slip. I tightened the clutch, using my spanner frozen-fingered in the teeth of the wind, but to no avail. The pressure of the wind was too great and the vane jumped straight out again.

And this, I knew, was to be the continuing story of the novice who was going to try to go through the Roaring Forties in winter in the wrong kind of boat. Once the sea had lifted the stern and thrown us catastrophically crablike, the rest followed automatically. I adopted the only course I could, lowering my sails and lying a-hull. Darkness came, and although I lit my hurricane lamps – having decided a few nights previously that ploughing unilluminated through the night needed stronger nerves than mine – I could think of nothing I could usefully do. So I went to bed and left the South Atlantic to its own devices.

My intention was to stay there for a couple of hours and then get back upstairs to re-set the sails if there seemed any sign of improving conditions. I set the alarm, snuggled down – and did not awaken until 0700 hours. By that time, I was down to a force one whisper – and fog which limited visibility to two hundred and fifty feet. I knew I was still about two days away from Tristan da Cunha, but I was anxious for a sight. Without a sight, I might miss the island, which would leave me with the choice of wasting time by heading back north to find it or else pressing on for Cape Town and nullyfying all the letter-writing I had been doing with a Tristan postman in mind.

From lunchtime, the barometer dropped steadily until it was telling me what it had told me before the last gale. Its forebodings were fulfilled throughout the night. The sea and the wind rose together, the rains came, the rigging screamed stark defiance against a lightning-lit sky. I do not much go for lightning at the best of times – that is to say, on land and in the daytime. At sea and at night, it terrifies me. I can never forget that I am its only target. No grey dawn was ever more welcome than the dawn of the following day. By this time, I had taken to adding a pullover and thick socks to my efforts to combat the steadily dropping temperatures. Conditions outside were miserable, and they were not much better in the saloon because one of the results of having water in my petrol was that I had had to abandon any thoughts of using the paraffin cooker to keep warm with : paraffin's first duty was to the emergency lighting. Condensation was building up and everything was getting damp. In a way, I found myself envying the dozen porpoises which followed me for half an hour. At least, they seemed to be enjoying themselves.

Tristan became a reality at 0745 hours on Thursday, August 15. There it was, straight ahead of me, with barren, sheer cliffs and its top shrouded in cloud. It looked black and ugly, and I knew that the volcanic eruption of a few years previously had left uncharted reefs.

What it added up to, however, was that my navigation had turned up trumps, after all. It was probably going to take me all day to get there, but I immediately set about making my preparations with the new-found zip of an encyclopaedia salesman who had been invited to come in and wipe his feet. Not that I wanted to go in and wipe my feet. I did not want to touch land, because that would mean it was no longer a non-stop trip, and I still wanted to pull that off if I possibly could. But if I were to have a hope of doing so, I simply had to have fresh petrol which would enable me to charge the batteries for the radio which was my link with the world and for the lights to let the world see when I was coming. Being helped with petrol would automatically rule me out of the race, but that did not bother me : it would make it possible for Maureen to know where I was while I went on to satisfy my curiosity about the survival aspect of going global single-handed and without touching land.

If somebody would send out a boat from Tristan so that I could tell him my troubles and get some action, I would be happy.

Flares and anchor at the ready, ensign and burgee at the flutter, I went in closer. I was approaching land on my own for the first time – apart from the day I limped into Langstone Harbour after my sortie to the Nab Tower – and I was in uncharted waters.

It was a situation, I told myself ruefully, which was quite typically Blyth.

7

Tristan

Chay Blyth : August 15 – August 29

THE island top was shrouded in mist but there was no hiding the cliff faces which stared blankly at me as I edged my way closer with a wind freshening behind me. This, I felt, was a situation with all the promise of the seventh veil. I was about to tackle the mysteries involved in approaching land, a subject with which I was just about as unacquainted as I could possibly have been; I had an unchartered reef beneath me; and I had a lee shore ahead of me. If the wind became too uppity, *Dytiscus* could be swept ahead of it until she made cataclysmal contact with the rocks which were awaiting her. She would be smashed like an unwanted toy at the foot of the uncomprehending cliffs. And the cliffs would watch her destruction unmoved. I had a feeling it would be a performance which they had sat through more than once in their role as poker-faced observers of the possibilities open to the unholy trinity of wind, sea and rock.

I might not, of course, get as far as the base of the cliffs in any case. A submerged outcrop might scythe through my barnacled hull at any time. If it did, I would take to my life raft and hope that I was not blown right past Tristan.

I was about half a mile off shore and I thought I could make out some houses. No sign of life, though. Still, you do not see signs of life on the Isle of Wight either. But the Isle of Wight is not like this : it's green and friendly, not tall and gaunt and waiting for your first mistake.

In closer.

Depth gauge showing bottomless, but a sudden shelf can alter that, no trouble at all. Yes, that's the village, right enough. Edinburgh, it's called – and that's the homeliest thought of the morning. Is that a white boat ahead?

Closer ,closer. Flares and life raft ready. Radio telephone on 2182.

I should have thought somebody would have seen me by now.
That boat is breakers on a reef.

And now, a great swell is beginning to build up. Perversely, I
find I am enjoying myself. I am approaching the unknown with the
excitement of an urchin encountering an unopened parcel. This is
worth losing two days for, quite apart from the object of it all,
which is to seek the petrol that will enable me to tell Maureen where
I am and to try to get my letter posted. I feel suddenly buoyed up and
tingling. *Blyth, you're crackers.*

Now there seems to be some sort of fishing boat not far from the
shore, with its bow high and its stern low. I wonder if it will have
any spare petrol for me . . . .

This time, it really *is* a boat, a biggish one, and it's flashing a
signal which I cannot make out.

Send up first flare. It's a big decision to have to make, because a
flare means a ship in distress. I am not in distress, but I have got to
make somebody see me somehow.

Back to the receiver, hoping that there is enough in the batteries
to see me through the next few minutes. *Dytiscus* rolls impatiently.

There is a hiss and a crackle as my radio clears its throat. Then
it speaks – with the voice of Tristan Radio. Introductions. Then the
news I have been waiting to hear.

'You are all right where you are. There are no reefs near you.
The other vessel is the *Gillian Gaggins,* from South Africa. It is
sending a small boat out to meet you.'

As I sailed in further, I peered through the grey afternoon, ready
for the first sign of the advance party. It was not long before I saw
it, phutting through the waves in my direction – a motor boat and
two seamen. Twenty minutes later, they were alongside me and we
were shouting salutations above the noise of the engine. The seamen
in charge – a small, tough, darkly tanned citizen in a checked shirt –
was cheerfully intent on coming in close to *Dytiscus,* and I had to
tell him to keep clear because I had visions of an unhelpful collision.
In broken English, he said that there was nowhere safe for me to
anchor close to the shore : it would be best for me to lay in to the
stern of *Gillian Gaggins.*

I followed the boat in to within fifty feet of the ship, then I
dropped sail and threw a line which one of the seamen fastened to the
ship. The black crew and five white officers were at the rail, all
looking very serious as they peered over at *Dytiscus* bobbing at her

unconventional anchorage.

The captain, Neil MacAlister, was a medium-built Scot with a lean, tanned face and fair hair. He introduced himself from aloft, and invited me to go aboard, plainly intent on doing anything he could to help me. Even as I hesitated, I was telling myself that it seemed ridiculous to be prepared to accept petrol from him if he offered it and yet to refuse his offer of hospitality. Here we were, two Scotsmen in the middle of the Atlantic, and he was asking me aboard for a dram : how could I say that it was not possible?

I thanked him and explained my situation, plus the fact that I did not want to go ashore. If he was boggling a bit at the difference between coming aboard a ship for petrol and going on land for petrol, he was boggling discreetly. The Diplomatic Corps would have been proud to acknowledge him. But when he began saying what *he* was doing at Tristan, I am afraid I was unable to follow his example of imperturbability in the face of the incredible. I gasped like a novice in a sauna bath and I made no bones about it.

Gillian Gaggins had arrived from Cape Town only that morning, and she would be leaving the following day – as soon as she had pumped fuel to the island. Moreover, this was a job which she carried out only three times in a year.

It was all entirely unbelievable. He said it did seem pretty lucky, whichever way you looked at it. My arrival had coincided with his, in the face of odds of about a hundred and twenty to one against, and here he was with a ship which could give me the very stuff I was looking for.

I shook my head. This was more than luck. Coincidence alone could not take the credit. God had been a reality to me throughout the trip, and now, yet again, He had manifested His presence. I was totally shaken, utterly torn between gratitude and disbelief.

It was time, however, for the practicalities. The chief engineer, Arthur Leeder, came aboard *Dytiscus* and took an expert look at the generator. He said it would take about three hours to fix it because of the rust which the sea water had caused, and he suggested that it should be taken aboard *Gillian Gaggins* so that he could strip it completely in his workshop. The only problem he foresaw was that if I used the fuel which *Gillian Gaggins* was carrying I might get some oiling-up of the plugs. I assured him that this was something I would be happy to learn to live with : what mattered was that the generator was going to work again.

After making sure the decks were clear, with sails away and firmly lashed, I went aboard *Gillian Gaggins* by way of the door in the side of the ship through which the islanders pass their boatloads of crayfish bound for South Africa. The crew still had not got used to the idea that they had found a jester in a little boat from the other side of the world, and I had run the gauntlet of helping hands and transparent disbelief.

Neil MacAlister introduced me to his wife and officers – and he gave me a piece of news which nearly made me choke on my whisky. He had read in a South African newspaper that John Ridgway had had to put in to Recife and was out of the race. After that, we spent an hour talking round a whisky bottle, debating the possibilities which could have led to John's withdrawal.

Then I discovered that *Dytiscus* had clouted the stern of the ship and had emerged from the impact with a pulpit rail – that is the metal handrail over the bow – which was impressively bent. I moved the yacht to an Admiralty anchorage nearer the shore, where bigger boats than *Dytiscus* had ridden out storms before now. I attached three lines to the anchor line, satisfied myself that all was secure, and returned to *Gillian Gaggins* aboard a ship's boat.

While I treated myself to a shower and washed my hair, I compared the way things had worked out for me with the news that Neil had given me about John. I felt completely stunned. Somehow, I had never thought that anything like that would really happen to either John or to myself. After all, we had survived the Atlantic in an open rowing boat. As I towelled myself, I had to agree that this did not, on reflection, seem the most logical sort of reasoning – but until now I had never thought of doubting its reliability. I suddenly felt uncomfortably vulnerable: perhaps something had gone wrong with John's boat – and if something could go wrong with John's boat, something could go wrong with *Dytiscus,* too.

Things, I now realized, could no longer be regarded as being likely to happen only to somebody else: I had no built-in unsinkability, nothing special that would make me float where others foundered. Yet this had been the insupportable premise on which I had been working so far. Blyth, I said, just watch it.

I felt the least I could do was to send John a telegram : 'Sorry to hear of sad news. But as you once said, nothing is worth dying for. Hope to see you when I get back and all four of us can have dinner. Chay.'

I awoke next morning to the hum of the ship's engines, which was something I had not expected. I dressed quickly and shot off to see what was happening. A look at the falling barometer, the rising sea and the force eight – 34 to 40 knots – gale made it hardly necessary to ask. Neil had decided to move away from the inner ancrorage and wait for calmer conditions : this was no day for staying in close and pumping fuel to Tristan. It meant that I was stuck on board for an extra day, but this did not matter and *Dytiscus* seemed to be riding well. I took the opportunity to write some letters and get my burn attended to.

Tristan Radio had a telegram for me from Maureen, dated July 18 – a month old. It told me that Robin Knox-Johnston was ahead of me. I was told he was at 25° South 15° West and about eight hunded miles behind me, but I knew he would be in front again if I did not get back on board pretty quickly. It also reported that the draft lease on Ropelawshiel was through and answered my doubts about what the weather was doing to the base of the yacht's mast :

'Eye on mast aluminium. If eyebolts through mast gunmetal no worry corrosion round latter. Little stress this point. Thank you, Daddy, birthday wishes. All is well. Yours forever. Metrobeale.'

I sent a telegram to Maureen straight away.

'Seawater in bilge. Needed petrol for radio and lights. Called Tristan. Did not go ashore. Letter and logs on way. Heard John has given up. Can you confirm? What news others? Reply Cape Town Radio. Missing you both. All my love. Metrobeale.'

I conjured up an equally impressive one for Ronald Nierop :

'Water in bilge amongst petrol. Created problems. Received petrol from ship. Did not go ashore. Rudder shaft rises about one inch. What do you suggest is wrong and what action? Letter on way. Repy Cape Town Radio.'

Frank Allen also came in for the full treatment :

'Position 37 South 12 West. Water in bilge amongst petrol. Created problems no communications, distress or lights. Received petrol form ship. Did not go ashore. Letter on way. If have to put in will want Maureen to fly out. Could you help organise? Hope to see you Needles April time. Reply Cape Town Radio.'

Reading that lot through, I felt that Blyth had gone something of a bundle. It almost made the letter-writing to which I now settled seem a superfluous exercise.

The exercise which became necessary the next morning, however, was alarmingly essential: I was having breakfast with Neil Mac-Alister, his wife and Arthur Leeder, when the coloured bosun burst upon us with the air of a bosun who had something on his mind. He did not keep me in suspense.

'The yacht's broken loose! You're going to lose it if you don't move quickly.'

I yipped like a stepped-on puppy, then I dashed with Neil and Arthur to the bridge. I could not think what I could expect Neil to do: there was a force seven wind and the sea was heaving like an affronted prima donna. *Dytiscus* was tossing on the swell, revelling in the new-found freedom which seemed certain to end with her being crumpled on the waiting rocks.

'Neil', I shouted. 'What the hell can I do? You can't possibly put a boat out to sea like this, and it's far too rough for me to swim – but I've go to get aboard somehow.'

I yammeerd a bit more. Neil did not say much. If he was thinking sombre thoughts about amateur sailors who cannot even be relied upon to moor a pint-sized yacht, he kept them to himself as he went coolly, professionally, about the business of getting *Gillian Gaggins* under way. Now that my first sensation of panic was over, I had had time to realize that the wind was from the south-west and that *Dytiscus* was in fact being blown away from the island: she was not going to be smashed after all – just taken out to sea to press on without me. It would give the Royal Southern people something to think about if they saw her coming up the Hamble in six months' time. Look-no-hands, sort of thing.

Neil had by this time formulated his plan.

1. Second Officer: prepare a lifeboat and brief a crew.
2. Chief Officer: arrange a grappling party, with a line long enough for towing.
3. Blyth: keep out of the way.

The idea was that we should go up wind, drift down on *Dytiscus,* throw a grapple and tow her round to the lee of the island. There, the boat would be lowered and I could be shovelled aboard with my precious petrol and the other things that Neil had let me have – some varnish and paint, a paintbrush, two torches, some magazines and a tin-opener. I was particularly delighted about the tin-opener. The plan sounded simple enough, but even I could see that it was not going to be as straightforward as all that. Manoeuvring a thousand-ton ship in what was by this time a forty-knot gale, so that it came alongside a yacht which was keeling and cavorting like an apache dancer on pep pills, was hardly the sort of job for which you could hope to open a seamanship manual and find it coming up with full instructions on page twenty-six. Neil, I could tell, was a bit worried. I resolved to stick firmly to the position he had allotted me in the plan of campaign.

Now, calmly and efficiently, Neil began to give orders, and *Gillian Gaggins* started to circle the writhing yacht. We went round three times, while the affronted sea hammered foaming frustration from bow to stern. The first circuit was a trial run. Second time round, the grapple was thrown overboard but the rope aboard *Dytiscus* which came into its clutches slipped free after the briefest of captivities. The third time, she was ours, firmly in tow behind us. Jeff Dominy, the chief officer, had obviously made a good job of briefing his native grappling party : *Dytiscus* came to heel unhurt. Then, with the yacht following like an obedient puppy, we moved round to the other side of the island, where it was much calmer.

There, I shook hands with Neil before climbing into the lifeboat with the second officer and three members of the crew, to be lowered over the side. We made the short trip to *Dytiscus,* and I took my petrol and other supplies aboard while the lifeboat returned to the ship. I stowed everything safely away, hoisted the storm jib and moved past *Gillian Gaggins*. As I did so, I saluted Neil by lowering and raising the burgee. While everybody on deck waved, he gave an impressive performance on the foghorn. Within an hour, the ship that had solved my problems was out of sight.

Sunday, August 18, totally failed to depress me, although it did its best. After a bitter, blustering night, it brought rain and hailstones that came like rattling curtains, bouncing high off the saloon roof and doing their utmost to give the deck a white carpet despite the way the sea kept coming aboard and washing them all away. I pushed on with the storm jib and two reefs in the mainsail, with the boat going chin-up for one towering mountain after another and the cold giving me hands I could not feel as I struggled to keep some control over my wayward canvas.

But everything was bearable from 1100 hours onwards. This was when I made contact with *Gillian Gaggins* and they passed on a telegram from Maureen. It read :

'S.F. (Samantha Fiona) walked 13th. Use petrol for lights. Ignore radio. Use M.I.K. If at all possible try finish in one. What do you say – never give up. Keep moving Dytiscus, kep moving. Metrobeale. I will toast you 0800, 26th. We love you for ever. Prayers work miracles. Maureen.'

I knew Maureen, of course. I knew that hers was a loyalty which could always be counted on to shine like an undipped headlight. But even so, this telegram fairly made me stagger with a new awareness of the extent to which she was prepared to back me in this mad, mad merry-go-round on which I was embarked. I had got petrol purely and simply so that I could radio my positions for her sake – and she was sitting at home and saying I should ignore the radio. A woman in a million. I was out of the race because I had been helped, but she was insisting that I should still try to make the circuit without touching land. She did not want me to give up; she was not expecting me to give up. How could I let such loyalty down, There and then, I resolved that I would not give up just as long as my game little boat seemed able to go on taking its punishment; just as long as the exercise did not become so hazardous that to go on would be sheer folly. Widowhood at twenty-four would be a rotten return for an investment of faith such as hers. Not, of course, that I would be in a hurry to make even the least worthy of wives a widow : I am a great believer in hanging on to me, despite the periodic episodes which give my friends cause to wonder.

My reply to Maureen was :

'Congratulations to S.F. Wish I was there. 0800 hours 26th O.K. Biting cold and hailstorms. Almost lost Dytiscus. Details in log. Letters will take about a week. Will try not to give up, and thank you. All my love. Metrobeale. Chay.'

The next day, the weather did not improve, although it appeared to be trying to lull me into a sense of false security. Every so often, the winds would drop and leave me alone with the surging waves. But then, without warning – wham ! It was like being clobbered with an invisible club, and for the next twenty minutes or so I would be at grips with a fury which was frighteningly unfettered. If ever I had been caught with a lot of canvas up, I am sure it would have been ripped away. As a day for a sail, it was a non-starter.

On the other hand, as a day for telegrams, it was in a class of its own. At 0900 hours, *Gillian Gaggins* passed on a signal from Frank Allen :

'Can you carry petrol in plastic containers? Is ship still around? You have made fantastic time. Don't push her too hard. My assistance is always here for any circumstance. I back any decision. You are well in lead. King still here. Frank.'

King was Cdr King, who was joining the round-the-world procession in his yacht, *Galway Blazer*. He was waiting in Plymouth and eventually left on August 23.

I replied:

'Many thanks reply. All is well now. Have petrol. Letter on way will take about a week. Dytiscus will take it. Standing up well. Chay.'

And I sent one to Isobel, my sister:

'Hope you enjoyed start. Blue and yellow flying well. Looking forward to next Common Riding. All is well but very cold. Regards to all. Hope to see you at finish if all goes well. Chay.'

And one to Clifford May, of the Holborn Sub-Aqua Club:

'Sorry did not see you before I left. It was all one last rush to get started. Hope to be diving with you again next summer. Regards to all. Reply Cape Town Radio. Chay.'

The sheer exhilaration of having my radio fit for active service again had made me for the time being forget that telegrams have a habit of requiring to be paid for. All day, my generator was hard at work. *P-p-p-p-p-p*. It was a sound which I had learned to hate before I lost it, but now, as I applied myself to my radio, it was the most beautiful sound on earth. *P-p-p-p-p-p*. It was as if I were setting my messages to music. Even the weather began to mend its manners, as if it wanted to stop and listen.

I took the opportunity to catch up on some maintenance: varnished the vane and quadrant, oiled the self-steering gear, aired and dried the carpet yet again, and both my sleeping bags. I reorganized the aft compartment, removing stacks of rations and putting them in the forward compartment to help the trim of the boat. I also packed my films in polythene to keep them away from the advance of condensation. I wanted to see the results of my efforts to fill the family album – because some of those efforts would have made a camera study in themselves. Taking pictures of the creatures of the sea and sky which occasionally brightened a dull day by coming to have a look at me was a fairly straightforward affair, provided I managed to click the shutter when the boat was steady. Taking pictures of me without a time-release mechanism was a different matter altogether.

It involved setting up the camera and tying one end of a long
piece of string round the shutter lever. Then I took the string over a
series of pulleys and tied the other end to my ankle. After that, it
was necessary to place myself in the line of fire and press on with
the shooting schedule for the day – Blyth shaving, Blyth drinking
coffee, Blyth writing a telegram – with a hopeful twitch of the
ankle coming at some time in the proceedings with a view to passing
the entire pantomime on to posterity.

I managed to maintain contact with *Gillian Gaggins* for another
four days. A telegram came from the Westfield Engineering
Company on Tuesday, August 20 :

'If water in keel, suspect breather. Plug when not in use. You
could shorten take-off pipe by two inches. If water in hull, suspect
upper rear corner anchor locker. To check, easiest re-seal hatch
itself. Some rudder lift normal when close-hauled. One inch rather
excessive but not dangerous. Rudder O.K. even without bottom
bearing. Suggest limiting lift by jurying from eye socket on rudder
to main bolts securing gear frame to deck. Congratulations and best
wishes. Westfield.'

I had, in fact, done most of the things suggested in that splendid
epistle. All the same, I found the reassurance about the rudder
made pleasant reading. It meant one worry less as I began my run-in
to the forties, shepherded by tremendous flocks of albatrosses and
petrels which stayed with me for an entire day. I varnished everything that was varnishable : if I were going in to the forties, I might
as well go in looking respectable.

I was also going in with a frenzy of rule-breaking. The winds
returned and built up to force six – 22 to 27 knots – and I had
developed the habit of putting up the mainsail and continuing to
run before them, without turning into them as I ought to have done.
It was a habit which necessarily gave me my full share of tricky
moments, but at least it kept me going ahead where luffing would
have lost me time. I knew I should not have done it, but I excused
myself with the thought that I should not have been there anyway.
I resolved to seek Nevile's views when I got home. I listened to the
ssssh-ssssh-ssssh of cloth on metal as the mainsail rubbed against
the stainless steel of the shrouds, and I went on running, utterly
unrepentant. A three-word telegram arrived from John Ridgway –
'Bon voyage. John' – and my little bit of rule-bending was helping

me to oblige.

I heard on my radio the news of the Russian invasion of Czecho-slovakia. I passed it on to the operator on *Gillian Gaggins,* who said they had not heard about it. 'It's going to be O.K.', I said. 'Harold Wilson's going to impose sanctions against Russia, and Rhodesia will go in as a neutral observer.' Apparently, that went down well with the South African officers on the ship.

That was Blyth being brave – trying to forget the forties which were waiting for him. I was trying to keep as close to an east course as I could : clipping the corner at the Cape of Good Hope would in fact keep me out of the forties, which struck me as an entirely commendable ambition. Sometimes I slipped south, sometimes north, but mainly I stayed somewhere between thirty-eight and thirty-nine degrees South, in the hope of eventually reaching the Indian Ocean without having actually sat up and begged for trouble.

In any case, there was obviously plenty of trouble available in the thirties. The problem was the unpredictability of the winds. They would let me bowl along happily until I had got as far as thinking I could do with a bit more canvas so why did I not take out the refs from the mainsail – and then, with about three seconds' warning, they were on me. To receive the warning, I had to happen to notice a patch of darker blue sea in the middle distance – a patch which had not been there a couple of minutes ago – or perhaps a low-lying mist made up of rain bouncing off the surface of the water. I knew then that the weather would be upon me in roughly two coughs and a spit – and sure enough, a tremendous gust would catch the vane with far more venom than the self-steering gear could cater for. After that, it was a panting, scrambling grab for the tiller and fight, fight, fight to get back on course while the wind, intent on keeping its advantage, buffeted the boat without a pause and the rigging screamed encouragement.

It was conditions like these which gave me my first experience of gybing, on August 22. Gybing is when the wind crosses the stern and the boom swings across to the opposite side of the boat until everything suddenly goes tight again with a tremendous *crack!* I had to get up at 0400 hours when one of these squalls from the south caught *Dytiscus* as we sailed on the port tack under storm jib and two reefs in the mainsail. I leaped sockless into a pair of welling-tons and dashed on deck wearing my sailing suit over nothing. It was hardly the gear for what turned out to be a two-hour performance in the dark, in winds which seemed to snap at my very bones.

And what a performance it was, heralded by an overture of rattling sails which flapped with the abandon of a chicken in a wind tunnel.

Disconnect the self-steering gear. Sheet in the boom. Slacken off the starboard sheet and preventer for the storm jib. Sheet in on the port side for the storm jib. Up and down, up and down on the swell for ten minutes, waiting for her to pick up way. After ten minutes, she is making about three knots. Hands, chilled and nerveless, to the tiller. Pull her round until she is running before the wind again. Gybe her back to her original course. Connect the self-steering gear. Disconnect the port sheet. Sheet in the starboard line. Slacken off the boom. Check course from the compass. Set the sails. Sheet in the preventer.

Even with a sail as unhungry as the storm jib, I was doing four knots, which was more than ample in these conditions of unpredictability. I was being forced north by a wind which was just east of south, but I did not mind that : it was still winter and I was in no hurry to go south.

What did bother me was my equipment, some of which was showing signs of wear. The eye on the wire halyard of the mainsail looked as if it was getting ready to part, so I made one of my 'preventers'. I fastened it to the halyard from a strong point on the deck beside the mast, and I hoped that when the crunch came it would hold firm : if it did not, I would be doing my Christmas tree fairy act at the top of the mast again.

The spindle from the reefing handle came out and went over the side, so I made a substitute from a screw and hoped for the best. And I used some spare rope and a shackle to make a new jib sheet to replace the one I lost when *Dytiscus* went adrift at Tristan.

In a way, I was glad to have something to take my mind off my surroundings. I was becoming more concerned each day about what *Dytiscus*'s prospects might be when this apprehensive piece of ocean eventually lost patience and hurled a screaming green hell at me. A less welcome distraction was my right wrist, still troubling me where I had burned it on the pressure cooker two-and-a-half weeks previously. At one stage, it had developed a five-by-four inch blister, and now it was playing up after being soaked in salt water. Even bathing it with fresh water failed to ease it. With my fingers beginning to be covered in salt water sores, which were not painful but

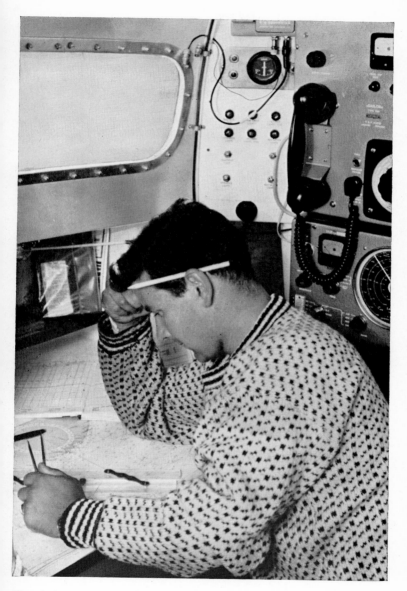

Chay is lost very soon after leaving the shores of England.

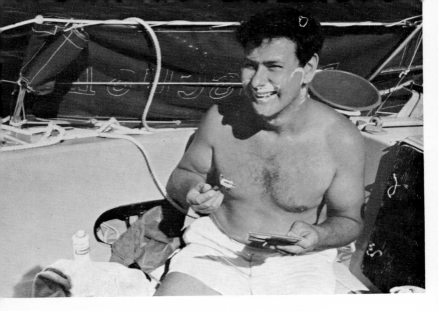

In the tropics the cockpit was splendid for Chay's regular shave.

Further south it meant oilskins on deck.

which would hardly have got me into a Fairy Snow advertisement, I was about as unprepossessing a prospect for a handshake as you could imagine.

I had a fright when I was faced with a rising gale and discovered that the boom appeared to be broken. For a moment or two, I was as bewildered as a gardener who has gone out to plant sweet peas and has found he has struck oil. But when I had steeled myself to taking a closer look, all that seemed to be necessary was a firm shove to push it back into its holder, where it had to marry with the reefing gear. After that, I had to give a repeat performance about every five days.

One way and another, there was plenty going on between squalls. I lost a spanner to a rogue wave which took me by surprise when I was fixing a retainer on the mainsail. My shaving mug went the same way when I was rinsing it after shaving. 'Blyth', I said sadly, 'it'll be you next.'

I sorted out all my bedding and put it to air upstairs, turning *Dytiscus* for the nonce into a cross between a switchback and a Chinese laundry. I painted the compass and self-steering gear brackets, an exercise which confirmed how right I had been to entrust all the pre-trip varnishing to Maureen. I gave myself a haircut, a painstaking effort with ragged results, but one which I decided had effected an improvement on Blyth unbarbered. And I began to do unplanned things like drinking tea without sugar and milk, and tipping the contents of a packet into my waste bucket and keeping the packet. I found that my eggs, six dozen when I started, were down to sixteen.

It was an edgy, uncertain time. Gloomy foreboding was having a field day as I moved about my daily duties. All I could be confident about was that one day in the fairly immediate future I was going to be put precipitatingly through my paces; and that this would be the signal for a battle which would continue for however long it took me to sail my brave little boat out of this angry area – or for however long it took for *Dytiscus* finally to submit to the effects of a catclysmal hammering of a kind her makers had never contemplated. The signal came on August 28, at 0330 hours.

The previous night, I had gone to bed bewitched by the sunset There was one small cloud in front of the sun, and this had become the apparent source of a glory of red and golden rays which warmed the vaults of heaven and shimmered its own responses across a mirror

D

sea. It was a soft-centred sunset; a sunset without a sun and with only one spectator – me. The rigging creaked in a different breeze. Below, I heard my tins stirring. My bow wave hissed against the hull. These were the sounds of silence; of a glowing, magical peace. I drank it the way I drank my coffee, to its dregs. And as darkness crept about me I went down below, leaving my mainsail and ghosting genoa to take me through the night at a gentle three knots.

I was awakened by the angle of keel, which eighty-one nights at sea had taught me to recognize subconsciously as a sort of built-in alarm. I scrambled into my sailing suit, poked my head outside, checked my course with the compass in the cockpit, and realized that I was crashing crazily through the night to the north-west – exactly the opposite direction to the one I wanted. A wild wind thrashed the darkness as I fought to lower the sails and to get back on course. The deck was slippery with water which had made its escape from the heaving turublence surrounding the yacht. The rigging, which had whispered to the sunset, was whistling like a continental football crowd.

Two hours and twenty minutes later, after trying to contain the maelstrom with No. 1 and one reef in the mainsail, I was down to storm jib and a second reef and was careering north-east. And two hours after that, when the wind changed from south-east to south, I began to nose due east with two warps over.

That day, a contact with Cape Town Radio brought me a telegram from Clifford May, of the Holborn Sub-Aqua Club 'Delighted: to receive your telegram. Our thoughts and concern are with you and Maureen each day of your journey. May God help your courage and bring you back safely to home port.'

I echoed that prayer. In the grey dawn of battle, my reefing gear had come apart as I had struggled to come to terms with recalcitrant canvas. In the end, I managed to drop what little of the mainsail I still had up and I set the trysail. For the rest of the day, *Dytiscus* took the fury of winds which changed from force nine only in order to become force ten – anything between 48 and 55 knots. There was no respite, hour after buffeting hour. And at 0400 hours next day, after the seas had thrown the boat sideways, the self-steering gear slipped and gave me something else to think about for the following sixty minutes.

By mid-day, the final shots of that first skirmish had been fired.

With the certainty of more and bigger battles to come, I began to repair the mainsail. And I prayed the prayer of a lone sailor who was beginning to realize what he had let himself in for.

8

Make or Break

Chay Blyth: August 30 – September 13

THE next few days, I knew, were to be the make-or-break days. If *Dytiscus* and I could go on taking what was coming to us, nothing would stop us afterwards. For forty-eight hours, I had had to run with the gale and had been forced well to the north-east, and now – thanks to a change in the wind while I was asleep – I was going south-west. Three days of reconnoitring a landscape of mountains and canyons which was always changing and yet always the same had given me a course like a crocodile's tooth. I was frightened, cold, depressed; cursing the pointlessness of the whole miserable exercise, the same as I had cursed the pointlessness of rowing the Atlantic with hands locked claw-like to those interminable oars. From the beginning of the trip, I had prayed each night: now I began to pray each morning as well.

At noon on August 30, I was at 38° 34' South, and I was beginning to doubt if I would ever reach the forties. Every time I seemed to be making my run-in, a gale would throw me north again – and by midnight yet another one was upon me, again from the south.

Throughout that night, the battle was on again. Monstrous white-capped sea hills as high as my mast surged out of the darkness, each one advancing as *Dytiscus* shivered under the hail of icy covering fire which had erupted from the sonorous crash of the one before it. And at 0400 hours, one of them nearly got me. I was sitting just aft of the mast, fitting the trysail, when a wave roared aboard and clouted me clean across the saloon roof. The boom failed to stop me because the impact had wrenched it out of its reefing fitting. For a wild, panicking eternity which must have been all of a tenth of a second long, I careered spreadeagling through the flying spray. Then I stopped with a jerk which had me choking breathless relief and disbelief as I reached the limit of my safety line. For a moment or two, I just lay there, flexing grateful fingers in a puddle as the hail of needles swept over me. *Oh, God, am I still here?*

I got to bed at 0630 hours and was up again at 1000. *Dytiscus* was still taking all that a forty-five-knot gale could throw, but she shuddered desperately every time a galumphing wave came at her with the urgency of the Bournemouth Belle on its home run to Waterloo. Again and again, grey-green sheets rose to claim her, each one a potential shroud. Again and again, she shook them off with a terrifying roll which made all my stores contribute clangorously to the uproar. And doggedly she crabbed her way up the next hillside before pitching without pause into the valley beyond.

The spray-dodgers – canvas awnings meant to protect the cockpit – gave up the struggle: nine-poundsworth of protection simply ripped to pieces. Then yet another rolling colossus hit its target, swinging the yacht round something like fifty degrees. How the self-steering gear could take it, I could not imagine.

Every gale, and there were plenty of them, made its mark. Sometimes, probably because I was becoming a bit punch-drunk, I inadvertently added a bit of destruction of my own. I managed to fix the downhaul for the trysail into an electric cable, gave a mighty pull, and disconnected the masthead light and spreaders. The spreaders are the lights which are fixed to the crossbeams on the mast and illuminate the deck.

And every gale helped to push me north. I was within three hundred miles of Cape Town without a mast light and likely to be meeting shipping quite soon. That was a sobering sort of thought. On September 1, I was 37° 32′ South, 15° 10′ East, and there was not a sign of a wind from the west or the north. The forward compartment roof began to leak, as if impelled to show its active support for all the other spots which were admitting the Atlantic. It had never struck me until now that a colander could float. Leak-locating was particularly problematical because *Dytiscus* was double-skinned: by the time the water was through the inner wall, it could have come from anywhere.

Monday, September 2, brought me a link with Cape Town Radio via a ship called *Swazi*. Over the air came a telegram from Maureen, packing the advice she had been garnering about my petrol problem. 'Siphon petrol from boat by clean rag. Rag will hold water. Petrol will pass through. Leave to strain three times. Clean rag each time then put petrol in cup. Water will come to top if not strained properly. May not work with salt water. Worth a try. Keep moving, Dytiscus, non-stop.'

They were words of wisdom which had come too late, but their arrival served as yet another reminder of the faith of the girl I had left behind. I could feel her willing me on, on, on. Keep moving, *Dytiscus, non-stop. Maureen, sweetheart, I'm going to try like hell.*

I was becoming aware of a shortage in my canvas armoury. I wanted a sail to fill the sequence gap between the No. 1 and the storm jib. The absence of a No. 2 was costing me miles. The No. 1 would carry me forward at six knots, but if the wind then increased I had to hoist the storm jib and accept a reduction to three knots, whereas a No. 2 would have enabled me to maintain speed.

These were lamentable sailing days. If I did not have a gale, I had calms and squalls in rapid succession. I had learned to spot a squall coming by the colour of the sea on the horizon. When I did so, the drill was to head down wind – and off course – then let out the sails a little and wait for it to have its fling. When it had passed me by, I had to re-set the sails, get on course and re-set the self-steering gear. It does not sound too much of a problem, but its charm tends to fade a bit when you have done it every twenty minutes for a whole day.

A noon sight on September 3 put me at 38° 25′ South, 18° 30′ East, which was a minor disaster in itself since it meant I had covered only a hundred and sixty miles in two days instead of the two hundred and forty I could theoretically have expected.

The reason was my reluctance to let the winds catch me unprepared for their onslaughts : I pressed on with two reefs in when I could have had the mainsail up. I sailed with the wind I expected, with the wind I had not got – and sometimes the wind I expected did not come. I watched a school of a hundred dolphins, and I envied them their independence of these inconsiderate conditions.

This was the second anniversary of my landing with John on the Aran Isles, and it was a similar sort of day – prone to come along with an occasional mini-gale to make sure that there was not much chance of boredom setting in. A lone tern, the first I had seen since I left the Hamble, circled me for five minutes as an unexpected reminder of the pleasure which its fellows had given John and me on the days they had kept us company in the Atlantic. I wondered what John was doing now; wondered if he was back with the

Special Air Service; wondered if he had received the letter I wrote him earlier in the trip, before I heard he had given up; wondered if he would be at the finishing line if *Dytiscus* brought me through whatever it was these sly and savage seas had in store for me. I marked the anniversary as best I could, with a dinner consisting of scrambled eggs, rice and paella, and a packet of Smarties, while water broke over the saloon roof and ran down the windows to blur my view of the heaving landscape outside. I had two reefs in the mainsail. It was going to be a rough night. I remembered what we used to say in *Rosie:* 'The longer it lasts, the less it's got to go.' And I reached again for my Smarties and chobbled consolation. I was feeling very lonely.

My morale, in fact, was up and down with the insistence of a yo-yo on the finger of an expert. It did not take long for the boost of a good day to wear off. On the other hand, it was surprising how effective a good day could be if it arrived when I was eyeing my water-sodden world with unencumbered regret. Whenever I found another repair in need of my attention, I was filled with a despairing sensation that this was probably just the tip of the iceberg – that there were almost certain to be other jobs which wanted doing but which I had not found. But with each job done, I somehow found some extra zip, just as if my unavoidable sessions of do-it-yourself were what I needed to charge my personal batteries. I fixed the masthead light, re-sealed the anchor hatchway, sorted out some troubles on the self-steering gear, and tightened an eye-plate which had come lose at the base of the mast. And I felt all the better for it.

Day after day, I was knife-edged between dismay and delight. One day, for example, I was actually hoisting the mainsail when I was caught by a squall which had lurked entirely unsuspected until the moment it larrupped me. I panicked involuntarily, tried to pull the sail down again, and was horrified to see the boom jump out of the reefing gear again. My struggles to retrieve the situation served only to put an eighteen-inch tear in the sail and then prompted a batten to come out and fall overboard. I grabbed a second batten as it was about to follow suit – and proceeded to show the boom precisely what I thought of it by belabouring it for a good two minutes with the batten with which I was so fortuitously armed. Then the sheer stupidity of the situation came home to me, and, while the wind went on shrieking and the waves offered disaster every other minute, I joined in the crashing cacophony with gales of my own : gales of laughter.

But I yo-yoed again soon afterwards when I broke three needles before I managed to mend the sail. When I checked my position, I realized that this incident had been my introduction to the Roaring Forties : at 0830 hours on Friday, September 6, I was at 40° 15' South, 24° 25' East. Heaven help me, I was here at last.

The following day made my trip as long as the one across the Atlantic – ninety-two days. A brilliant sun sat in an almost cloudless sky and watched me trying conclusions with a force eight gale and horrendous seas – the biggest I had met so far, and typical of the forties, where the waves have unfettered opportunities to build up and up. Time after time, *Dytiscus* slewed sideways on to the mountain-sides which came at her in a curving crescendo of liquid hell. She writhed as tons of cascading calamity burst bomb-like against here, spewing foam-topped venom across the saloon roof and into the cockpit. With the thunder of the impact came the lightning : sunshine which sparkled a million times in the dancing spray. As I fought to hold the boat, I realized without any abiding appreciation that I had even acquired my own personal rainbow. We climbed sideways to a mountain top, plunged sideways into the cavity beyond; into a roaring gorge that was pregnant with fury. Keeling, crabbing, toppling, slithering, with as much say in our destiny as a matchstick in a waterfall, we reached the valley only to climb the precipice beyond.

At the top of each mountain, *Dytiscus* paused for a half-second eternity – time for me to take in the vista of a heaving sea. Then, with storm jib and trysail flapping frustration, we pell-melled into yet another terrifying trough of swirling spume.

In conditions like these, *Dytiscus* simply would not run. Time after time, she broached, making herself a sitting target for one monster wave after another. If anybody broaches in a sailing club, he goes back to the clubhouse and says, 'Hell, I broached!' And everybody says, 'God, he broached!' Then they all buy him a drink and they talk about it for the rest of the season.

I broached three times in one hour and eleven times in that one disastrous day – the only day it occurred to me to count. Other days, my score may have been more, it may have been less. And on the principle that talking does something for mangled nerves, I will be happy to talk about it for as many seasons as people are prepared to listen. I had embarked on this venture with no idea of what was waiting for me. Now I did know, and the discovery was shattering beyond description.

This same day, disaster became a tangible companion : the servo blade on the self-steering gear broke. I replaced it with my spare, but I could not bring myself to contemplate the immediate future with optimism. Broaching had caused the first blade to break almost as soon as I had entered the Roaring Forties : would the one I had substituted – my only spare – stand up to the many thousands of miles which lay in front of me? I very much doubted it. Heavy seas would almost certainly achieve the same result again – and if they did, I would have no alternative to steering by hand in the daytime and heaving-to at night. I was four hundred miles from South Africa, four thousand five hundred from Australia. If I risked it, and the blade broke when I was crossing the Indian Ocean, it would take me weeks to reach Australia. But if I played it safely I could be off South Africa inside a week and Frank Allen would be able to fly me out a spare.

I need not touch land : to that extent, I could still say it was non-stop, and receiving help would not matter because my petrol business had put me out of the race in any case.

What it amounted to was that the thing I was still curious about was me. The boat, simply because I had taken it where it had never been intended to go, had failed, in as much as it needed a repair job doing which I was in no position to do. But I still did not know if I myself could stand up to the circumnavigation – and if I could find out then I wanted to do so.

This business of making myself thoroughly unpleasant to the body which God gave me is something that has fascinated me for almost as long as I can remember. It is difficult to explain it, but I simply like to find out how much the human frame can put up with, and to see the sort of effects which are produced both physically and mentally as a result of prolonged loneliness under trying conditions. The whole thing is a bit like the man who hits himself on the head with a hammer because it's nice when he misses : I cannot say that I enjoyed my Arctic and desert survival courses or the rough parts of the Atlantic crossing any more than I can say I was enjoying having the stuffing knocked out of me in *Dytiscus III* – and yet there *is* an enjoyment, even if it is only of the relief when it is all over. And I did not want, if I could possibly help it, to miss finding out all I could about this round-the-world exercise simply because my boat was not able to do the thing in one go. Survival, after all, was the object with which I began my preparations, long before a newspaper came along and turned it into a race. Provided I could go on without being foolhardy, I wanted to see the thing through. It was my voyage of discovery, and what I wanted to discover was me.

I spent a couple of hours assessing the situation while I hung on to the tiller and tried to put some purpose into the path which the boat was following. I was trailing a couple of warps in an effort to slow my unpredictable progress, but I was still going far too quickly. If I could go slower than the waves, they would pass beneath me and do no damage, but when I was going faster than the waves, as I was now, I was a potential target for all they could throw at me. At any moment, the boat might turn nearly ninety degrees to the waves and come almost to a stop. The waves, on the other hand, would not stop – and the resultant collision would produce a shuddering catastrophe of noise and water to accompany the frenetic screaming of the rigging.

It is a bit difficult, I acknowledge, to find a reason why I should decide to go out of my way to give myself the opportunity of continuing to confront nature at its least lovable – but this is what I did do. I resolved to head for Port Elizabeth. There, I hoped, I would be able to pick up another servo blade before coming back into this raging maelstrom of wind-whipped seas. The only snag was that I had no charts of the area, and things might become unduly interesting if I found myself sandwiched between a gale and the shore. I could see no reasonable alternative, however : Port Elizabeth it had to be.

Having made my decision, I tried to establish contact with Port Elizabeth but failed completely. Then, as I recorded in my log, once again I was helped by Our Lord. Over the ether came the voice of Captain Koolof, of the Dutch merchant vessel, *Jongkind*. I told him my troubles – there is nothing quite like pouring out your heart in a raging gale – and gave him the two messages I wanted to send. He promised to pass them on for me, and I promptly went into my drowning-man-and-straw act.

Message number one was to Frank Allen :

'Servo blade broken. Suspect it will happen again. Can't take a chance with 12,000 miles of forties to go. Making for Port

Elizabeth. Hope I won't have to put in. I require two servo blades, selection screws for servo box, turned down drills for pivot bolts, two pivot bolts, three Walker's spinners and cord. Don't send till next message. May take a week. Can you assist? Reply Port Elizabeth.'

The other was for Maureen:

'Servo blade broken. Inform Westfield caused by running problem. Making for Port Elizabeth to pick up spare. Hope I won't have to get off. Frank will be sending. You send letter with it. Love you always am missing you both. Metrobeale. Reply Port Elizabeth.'

All day, while the sun just sat up there looking cosy and smug, *Dytiscus* tossed like a pancake on Shrove Tuesday. There was no respite, either for me or the boat. Twice, the cockpit was filled with its own surging, break-away sea, which sloshed about my thighs in a show of mini-sympathy with the turmoil outside. I offered a prayer of thanks for the inspiration which had prompted Ronald Nierop to make it good and deep: being in a cockpit which enabled me to soak from the thighs downwards gave me a far greater sense of security than I could have achieved if the water had been able to spill out once it had risen above ankle level. Not that any sense of security really had a hope of climbing above the barely perceptible once a quick peek to port or starboard had brought a reminder of the realities.

Tirelessly, remorselessly, mast-high mountains were on the march. It was quite ridiculous that I was here at all; utterly absurd that I should seek to draw comfort from the discomforts of partial immersion, as if the sea would have found the task of lifting me the extra foot or so over the side an insuperable difficulty, were it really to put its mind to it. I hung on in my cakewalk cockpit as my tough little boat pitched this way and that, a reluctant juggernaut thrown upon the mercy of a howling blue-green world. *Patience. Above all, patience.*

At the height of the storm the previous night, there was a heart-stopping moment when the mainsail halyard, which I had had cause to suspect seventeen days previously, snapped. I breathed again as I saw that my preventer was holding: had it not done so, another spell at the top of the mast would have been unavoidable. I spliced and whipped the new one in the dark, up on the heaving deck, and I burned the ends with a match to stop them fraying after putting them inside my anorak to shield them from the wind. It was a slow process which would not be hurried, and which was not accomplished before I had managed to burn my jumper as well. Then I taped the new rope to the broken wire and held my breath as I pulled the other end of the halyard and watched the joint I had made rising up the mast. If it came undone, all my efforts would have been in vain and I would be faced with mast-climbing without the option. I was also uncertain about whether the joint would be small enough to pass through the sheave at the top of the mast head.

Hesitantly, I pulled. The joint held. I pulled some more and watched as it rose towards the part of its journey which contained the key to my immediate future. It reached the sheave, came through without a hitch, and began its downward run. Thankfuly, I hauled it to me, separated the rope from the wire, fastened it to a shackle, and said my thanks.

It was not until nearly twenty-four hours later that there came the first signs that the fury was failing. Force ten became force seven. Force seven became force five. The mountains became mere hills. The hills became a diminishing swell. The rigging grew tired of screaming.

By nightfall, I was carrying all the sail I could and grumbling about the absence of wind while I went about mopping-up in conditions of calm. Some people, I told myself, are very hard to satisfy.

It was not hard, however, to find compensations. For this was a night which was silvery-still. It was a night for taking my stand behind my mug of coffee and watching a rippling sea adding a diamante hem to the star-studded dress which the heavens were wearing. The only sounds were the hiss of the bow wave and an occasional grunt of approval from some part of the now pacified rigging. An urbane moon seemed to plead her innocence of the savageries which had gone before. I looked, and I marvelled, completely overawed by the majesty of it all. On a night like this, alone with the wonders of God, it was easy to understand what it is that draws men to the sea. I was filled with a sense of the most perfect contentment and a readiness to accept my own utter insignificance in such a panoply of splendour.

Such nights are made for solo sailors – even solo sailors whose knowledge of the skies is as limited as mine. I knew, for example, that somewhere up there was the Southern Cross, but I failed to find it because I had omitted to discover what it looked like before I set off. I sipped my coffee and I tried to convert all sorts of star combinations into the Southern Cross, but I failed to find it. Not that it mattered : this was a night of oneness with nature, of giving a leg-up to the soul, rather than a night for sticking name-tabs on stars. The glories of creation were mine for the looking.

The following morning put an end to all that : I awoke and found I was pushing through fog. As if in compensation, I managed to make contact with Port Elizabeth, where a radio operator chortled like a turkey on Boxing Day when he found out that I had rowed the Atlantic. He had three telegrams for me. Maureen's, as usual, was packed to the eyebrows with reassurance :

'Everything ready for despatch Port Elizabeth harbour master. Still non-stop providing that you do not put in to port. Thinking of you always. Love you for ever. Metrobeale.'

There was one from Frank Allen :

'All parts located. Propose sending by air to harbour master Port Elizabeth. Await your instructions. Frank.'

And one from Westfield Engineering :

'Deeply sorry to hear of self-steering. Have you tried twin jibs, no main and weighted warp astern? Congratulations on progress and very best wishes for future. Westfield.'

That one tickled my imagination. I had the feeling that if I tried twin jibs when the wind was really blowing I would probably need a pilot's licence. I had used them a great deal in the Equator area with winds up to force six, and they were effective. But now, it was a different story. *Dytiscus* went very fast, but she yawed very badly, and it did not seem to matter whether I used twin jibs with number ones or storm jibs : the result was always another broaching.

Hereabouts, I found myself back in one of my recurring navigational tangles. I had come through two counter-currents at 39° South – on going east and the other going west, and because I was nearing land I was anxious to find exactly where I was. The prospect of putting a dent in Africa just did not appeal. I took two sights – my first for three days – and tried to obtain supporting evidence with radio direction finding beacons and my direction finding gear. The beacons send out signals which you have to check against your Admiralty list of signals and you take a compass bearing on them.

Consternation ! Each calculation put me in a different place, and the louder I did my sums the more alarming my situation seemed to become. I prowled backwards and forwards in a desperate search for enlightenment. I had been told that the forties were a navigator's nightmare because fatigue led to mistakes, and it was a piece of information I found utterly unconsoling. Anyone observing my restless pacing would undoubtedly have drawn a parallel between my air of despondency and that of a Roman lion who has just learned that they have run out of Christians – except that the average Roman lion might have been unlikely to have gone as far as to thump his head with his fist while shouting 'Seventeen and eight! What's seventeen and eight, for God's sake?'

The more I tried, the worse were the results. For forty-five minutes, I battered my head against the absurdity of it all, with near-panic making a pretty rotten partner for incompetence. *Where in God's name am I? What the hell is wrong?* Try my fingers. *Seventeen, eighteen, nineteen, twenty . . . .*

Pack up, you bloody fool. Pack up, and try again tomorrow.

Then I noticed that I had made my azimuthal projection south-west when it should have been north-east. Even Einstein would have had a job to get his sums right with that sort of starting point. I began again; achieved a minor delirium as everything fell into place – including me : my place, I found, was a hundred and eighty miles south-west of Port Elizabeth. Tomorrow, with any luck, I would be seeing the lights.

Once more, however, it was to dawn on me that when Rabbie Burns had held forth on the problems of plan-making he had splothered what is technically known as a bibful. The following day brought a forty-five-knot westerly gale and had me on parade with my storm jib, a trailing warp, and an uncomfortable inability to reduce speed below four knots. All day, it blew me east. A sight put me at 37° 17′ South, 28° 28′ East : I had already missed Port Elizabeth, and at the rate I was going there seemed every chance of my missing Africa.

And the folks back home were doing all they could to help : a telegram from Maureen announced that all the stuff I needed was on its way as requested – to Port Elizabeth.

* * * * * *

It is at times like this that I give praise for paratroopers. When one paratrooper finds that another paratrooper is in the soup and apparently about to go down for the third time, you can rely on him to do everything possible towards extrication. And with my spare servo blades and ancillary equipment heading for Port Elizabeth while I was now aiming for East London, two hundred miles up the coast, the paratrooper to whom I turned was a fellow Scot, Chick Gough.

Chick and I had joined the Parachute Regiment together in 1958, but he had subsequently come out of the Army to play football for Charlton Athletic. He was now living in Johannesburg with his Swedish wife, Lisa, and their two children, and his prowess with Highlands Park F.C. had made him South Africa's leading footballer. We had kept in touch with intermittent correspondence since he had emigrated.

I got through to Chick with my radio telephone, with my heart singing John Deacon's praises yet again. How I could have contemplated tackling the trip without a radio telephone, I just could not imagine. Yet that was what I had contemplated, and it was what I would in fact have done, had it not been for the fairy godmother generosity of this man who had been a complete stranger until the night he rang my front door bell and said he had come to drive me to Southampton.

I had already spoken to Chick once, before the weather had played havoc with my plans. I had had a link call to him via Port Elizabeth Radio for old times' sake. The discoverey that Blyth, his unpredictable buddy, was now making a clown of himself in the Indian Ocean had not come as too much of a shock, as I had told him of my plans in January, when he had called at my home during a visit to Britain.

During that first telephone call, he had rallied round with promises to meet me in Port Elizabeth and top up the servo blades consignment with a parcel of goodies. And now that I was telling him that Port Elizabeth was no longer figuring in my plans, he went on rallying unreservedly.

'Don't worry about a thing', he said. 'When all the stuff arrives at Johannesburg, I'll see about getting it re-routed to East London instead of Port Elizabeth.'

All that day, the gale and the sea kept up their terrible-twins act. The boat keeled disconcertingly before their ministrations. Every time I picked my way along the deck, I thought how much easier life would be if one leg were longer than the other.

But at about 2200 hours, conditions began to improve. By this time, I was fifty miles from East London. Five hours later, when Friday the thirteenth was still a babe in arms, I saw the light of Hood Point. By 0600 hours, I was four miles out and the wind had abandoned me completely. I contacted East London Radio and made arrangements for somebody to come out and meet me.

The noise of a diesel engine heralded the approach at 0830 hours of a forty-foot black launch, with 'Pilot' in big white letters on its side, chaperoned by a bubbling bow wave and followed by an ever-widening vere of irritated water. The pilot was an affably matter-of-fact character in uniform. One of his crew threw me a line, which I fastened to a cleat on the bow. And then I was on my way in. No yachtsman could ever have made a more audible approach than this one of mine, with *Dytiscus* skipping on the heels of its purposeful pathfinder.

South Africa in the early morning sunshine looked very pleasant as we made our way up-river. Admittedly the setting was not unlike London docks, but the green hills in the distance wer clean and inviting, and away to the right I could see hotels sitting just behind the beach. After half a mile, I tied up alongside a jetty, after which it was necessary for me to clear the customs, although the only thing I had to declare was my intention to export a couple of servo blades and a goodies pack. I explained to the pilot that I did not want to step ashore, and he approached the customs men on my behalf. They were very understanding: they not only came down to the jetty – they even let me have the sixpence to pay the duty stamp when they realized that I had no money.

I was adamant that I did not want to touch land – and yet, as I stood on deck saying my piece to the customs men, I could not help wondering whether in fact touching land would matter any more than going on board ship had mattered for John and me when we were at our lowest ebb in the Atlantic. We had said we could not possibly go on board ship: what would people say? But we did go on board ship and people said nothing. The world moves so fast that people really have no time to worry whether I go on board ship or stand on my head. It is in the newspapers one day, but it is forgotten the next.

And now, with reporters and sightseers lining the jetty to wish me well, or to invite me to dinner, or simply to stand and stare, I stuck firmly by my insistence that I must not touch land; faithful to a fetish which I knew did not matter a damn to anybody except to me and to Maureen.

It was quite ridiculous. For the sake of being able to say that I never stopped floating, I was turning up my nose at what would probably be the only chance I would ever have of seeing South Africa. I was on show like a monkey in a cage, a couple of feet away from the jetty. All that was missing was an offer of a banana.

It would make sense, I felt, to send Maureen a telegram telling her that the whole thing was off and asking her if she would leave Samantha with her mother so that she could fly out to join me. Then we could sail back to England together – and to hell with pushing pointlessly on round a world that didn't give a damn. Now that really *would* be the chance of a lifetime.

And yet, how could I? How could I let down all the people who had worked so selflessly to give a novice his chance to see the world non-stop? How could I cock a snoot at the efforts of Frank Allen, Chris Waddington, Bill Ridley, Neville Wood, Charlie Brooker and all the others? John Deacon had not had a holiday cruise in mind when he had spent five hundred pounds to fit me with a radio telephone. And Maureen, Maureen above all, would not expect me to give up. If I did, it would be a smack in the eye for all that loyalty of hers. All the same, if she were to fly out we could have a few days at Chick's place, then sail and sunbathe our way back to England . . . .

On the jetty, a happy, tubby little man is inviting me back for a meal and a shower. I say No, thank you, I must not leave the boat. He obviously cannot believe it; wonders where I have escaped from, and if he ought to put me back. *Hellfire, what a situation. Why don't people just leave me to my own stupidity?*

I twiddle with the ring which Maureen gave me when we became engaged. It is entirely hidden by tape because it broke when I dropped it in the cockpit in one of the weather's rougher interludes and there did not seem to be another way of mending it.

What would the patrons like their monkey to do next, I wonder. *What would they say about a monkey on a bucket . . . ?*

9

"Wouldn't it be Great . . . ?"

Chay Blyth : September 14 – October 7

I T occurred to me that a useful way of passing the time while I remained faithful to my self-imposed penance of not touching the land which was only a stride away would be to tape a message to Maureen. I attached my tape recorder to a battery, perched myself beside it, switched on and began to speak. Two dozen coloured observers sitting on the wharf were most impressed. If they had required further proof of the insanity of this visitor who had come so close to land but who would not now leave his boat, they must have felt that they had got it now that they could see me through the saloon windows, apparently talking to myself. I talked for twenty minutes, touching on everything I could think of. I described the way I had decorated the cabin, with the blue and yellow ribbons on the ceiling, the lucky white heather picture from the wrapping of a goodies pack on the wall, my parachute scarf and a line of Maureen's handkerchiefs by the window. I talked about my daily routine; about Samantha's birthday; about the pantomime of taking photographs of myself; about receiving the news of John Ridgway's departure from the race.

I told about the way I had managed to break the ring; about the bafflement which every radio operator expressed when he came to the Metrobeale bit in our telegrams. I said I would like to see a priest when I arrived back home.

'I have a lot of questions to ask. The only trouble is, this would have to be done very soon after I arrived back : in a week's time would be to late. It would have to be in the first few days. It's not often a chap has a chance to be alone as long as this. I would not even mind seeing a psychiatrist as well, just to see what it's all about. It's silly, really, not to take advantage of it . . . ."

I described the mountainous seas which had proved too much for the servo blade; threw in the assurance that I was not going to

114

do anything foolish.

'If at any time I think this yacht can't take it or there is something wrong, I shall not hesitate for any reason at all to put into port for repairs. If at any time I think it's too dangerous, then that's that.

'In no circumstances am I going to die for this. I want to spend my life with you and Samantha. Heroics are an absolute waste of time : in two days, I will be forgotten. I will appear in the obituaries column, people will say tut-tut, and that's it – and you are left to fend for yourself.

'It's my job to fend for you and be beside you, and that is where I am going to be . . . ."

The tape finished, I put in in its box and wrapped the box in a sheet of paper from a notebook, ready for posting. With so many sightseers asking if they could do anything to help, it should not be difficult to find someone who would not mind going in search of a pillar box.

The answer came sooner than I expected, with the arrival on the jetty of a group of members of the East London Sailing Club. The man who played postman was Andrew Hutcheson, whose yacht, *Granger,* was moored opposite *Dytiscus,* about three hundred feet away on the other side of the river. Another member of the party was Max Phillips, a former paratrooper in the Special Air Service and now an official of Veld and Vlei, which is the equivalent of Outward Bound. As I had been seconded as an instructor to the Eskdale Outward Bound School, in the Lake District, during my Army service, we were soon embarked on an acquaintance that had the most solid of foundations. Max agreed to winch me up to the top of the mast so that I could see what was had been happening up there in the last few months. I wanted to make sure that there were no pins coming loose and that the masthead was not fractured; to see that no wires were corroded too badly; to check that there was no damage to the metal tangs which stick out from the mast-head to support the stainless steel forestay and backstay.

I got out the bosun's chair from the aft compartment, and as Max applied himself purposefully to the winch I began my ride upwards. It did not take me long to ascertain that Charlie Brooker's back garden efforts were still holding good. I was perched up there, feeling good in the afternoon sunshine, when I was aware that the activity on the jetty below sudden included a familiar tall figure in sports jacket and dark glasses.

'Hello, Chick', I said, and he flipped me a casual wave in return. It was as if we were in the habit of exchanging curtesies every day. Certainly, nobody who saw our exchange would have suspected that the last time we had been together had been nine months ago, when he was back in Britain for a few days and visited Maureen and me in Portsmouth.

'I've got a bottle of whisky in the car', he called. 'Shall I bring it?'

He did not really need an answer to that one, but Igave him one anyway. Five minutes later, we were down below, with Chick's powerful frame spilling along the bunk and his long legs stretching out across the floor, loose-limbed and casual. I produced a couple of mugs while he found his way into the bottle. I held them as he poured. 'Cheers', we said. The formalities thus completed, I plonked my backside on to the other end of the bunk and sat back contentedly to contemplate the amiable character who had taken a week's holiday from the job that he had outside football to try to help me out of the problem of being at East London, while all the spares were addressed to Port Elizabeth, two hundred miles away. He had arranged that everything would be re-directed as soon as it reached Johannesburg, so all I had to do was wait. There was going to be no need for me to disobey my own rule about not going ashore : I had decided that South Africa was out of bounds, and thanks to Chick it could stay out of bounds. Not for the first time, my heart gave praise for ex-paratroopers.

'How's it going then, Chay-boy?'

The familiar Scots accent was a joy to hear. I said that just at the moment things were not going at all, only I said it a bit more briefly than that and I pulled what Maureen calls my disgusting expression. I unended my mug. Chick summoned the bottle to action again.

The day wore on. Early in the evening, Chick popped ashore and returned with some bottles of beer and two enormous portions of fish and chips whose aroma curled gloriously round my nostrils. I put one of my tapes of Scottish music on the tape recorder.

Fish and chips, whisky, beer, bagpipes and nostalgia : it was quite a mixture. We remembered the old times, like when we were at Aldershot swimming baths, taking our swimming tests during our basic training. Chick had been a learner, and as such he had had to go backwards and forwards on waterwings. The incongruity of the sight he had presented – a big, hard paratrooper relying on a couple of baby bagfuls of plastic buoyancy – had made quite an impression on us at the time. And now, with the memory coming to the surface in a sort of alcoholic technicolor, we were all the more appreciative. Then there had been the occasion, before I had met Maureen, when Chick had brought his Swedish wife, Lisa, to my home in Hawick for a week's holiday during our annual leave. Lisa said that if the three of us were going out that night she would need a pair of nylons. Chick and I set off at 10 a.m. to buy a pair, leaving Lisa at home. One thing somehow led to another, as they always seemed to do when Chick and I were together, and we were missing from the domestic scene for the next six hours, until we fell out of a taxi and staggered in riotous uncertainty over the doormat. We never did get out that night – but somehow along the line Chick had at least managed to remember the nylons.

It now occurred to us that it would be a good idea to call Lisa, who was at home in Johannesburg. We did so, each of us taking a turn at the radio teelphone to give her an exuberant Hello.

It was growing dark outside. By now, we had seen off Chick's whisky bottle and had to grips with one of the Dewar's from my own supply. We were feeling pretty good.

It was Chick who made the remark that was to have all the repercussions.

'Wouldn't it be great if we could think of an adventure for the pair of us . . . ?'

I beamed. This was ridiculous. Here was I, only half way through one harebrained undertaking, and Chick was wanting to steer me into another one. But he was quite right : *wouldn't* it be great . . . ?

'Chick, you're a genius! Have another drink . . . ."

After that, the conversation pretty well looked after itself. We came up in turn with a whole range of possibilities. One of them was navigating through the Aberdare Forest in Kenya, on foot. This was the area of jungle, brush and swampland which had been the old Mau Mau stronghold. The idea of pushing through there had occurred to me when I was stationed in Bahrein, and for good measure I had wondered about climbing Kilimanjaro as part of the same trip. We mulled it over for a long time, but I was not happy about it. I like to try to do things *first,* not in somebody else's foot-steps, and to all intents and purposes the people who had spent so much time chasing the Mau Mau in and out of the forest had already killed this one as far as I was concerned.

'And anyway, Chick, I don't think we could get the maximum from it because it would not present too many problems. That sounds bloody stupid, I know. But if all those blokes have been there before us, it can't be all that impossible. I want something a bit more unlikely . . . ."

So we vetoed that one, as we vetoed several others when we put them up for judgment one after another. Then . . . .

'What about the Amazon?' I said.

It was inevitable, of course, that in any discussion of the sort on which we had embarked the Amazon would make an appearance. If you are really intent on looking for trouble, the Amazon can come up with all the mod. cons. Forests, swamps, headhunters, piranha fish, poison dart merchants. Who could ask for more? It offers vast areas of jungle where no outsider has penetrated because of the problems of navigation and of lugging enough food and other supplies for three months or more. The Indians there would probably be living on a minimum of food, of a kind which would not be acceptable to our sort of diet unless we happened to be at starvation point. And there were the psychological problems to be considered, as well as the physical ones.

'Let's have a crack at it', I said.

John and I had allowed our thoughts to stray to the Amazon when we were in *English Rose,* and now here it was again – rather more purposefully.

I fished in my chart locker and produced a South Atlantic chart which showed parts of South America, and we got down to the thing in earnest. We could travel about fifteen hundred miles up the Amazon in a steamer of some sort, to Manaus. Then up the Negro River by canoe or anything else that was available, perhaps as far as Tomar. Then we could cut south-west through the jungle until we reached another river, the Japura, which we could follow back to the Amazon, so that we would complete a circle.

But what would be the point of it all? Up a river, through a bit of jungle and down a river. So what? It was too aimless, too iry-fairy. And anyway, *most* people who went for the Amazon went up river. It was a bit old hat for our purposes.

'It's got to be down the Amazon for us', I said. 'We ought to start near its source, or from one of its tributaries on the west side of Brazil or Ecuador.'

Chick prodded the map. 'O here, in Peru somewhere . . . .'

We knew that Francisco de Orellana, a Spanish explorer, had set out to cross South America in the sixteenth century. The difference between him and us was that he had been accompanied by about two dozen other Spaniards, a huge contingent of Indian bearers and a string of horses, whereas all we would have was us. For us, the obvious thing was to get back to basics – to use the method which was the factor that had brought us together in the first place. Straight in, with no messing about – by parachute. We could bale out with a bergen apiece loaded to bursting point, then make out way down river by foot, raft or canoe. It was the obvious solution.

It did not take us long to realize that it was not; that it would be regarded as a gimmicky approach – as an easy way out of the problem of finding an easy way in. That was no good.

Chick found the answer. When he spoke, I could not think why it had taken us so long to get round to it. Our whole idea all along had been to pile the impossible on the improbable, and yet we had overlooked the obvious 'ideal'.

'Let's do the job properly while we're about it', he said. 'If we're going to do the Amazon down river, let's go over the Andes before we get there.'

I knew at once that this was what we had been looking for. To the headhunters and the piranha fish we could now add an eighteen thousand feet climb and the pleasures of height sickness.

I regarded my friend with undisguised delight.

'Terrific!'

After that, we really felt we were getting somewhere. We talked into the small hours of Saturday. Long after East London had gone to sleep, the bright eyes of *Dytiscus* were staring unwinkingly into the darkness. But eventually it was time for even *Dytiscus* to acknowledge lights out; time for the operations room into which her saloon had been converted to call it a day.

And in any case, we had finished the Dewar's.

* * * * * *

When we awoke, we breakfasted on the Avocado pears and cereal that Chick had brought with him, then Chick put on his track suit and disappeared for a run, leaving me exchanging civilities with sightseers who were as interested in the boat as they were in me. There are very few yachts in East London, so there was a general

enthusiasm for finding out all that there was to be known about
Dytiscus. People were also very keen to see if they could do anything for me. Some of them brought me Avocado pears and other
goodies. Several introduced themselves, like Eddie Baker, who
turned up with a pile of tinned food, and Mr Le Grice, who gave
me *Harpoon at a Venture,* by Gavin Maxwell, after learning that
I liked Scottish books. The newspapermen came back again, but
there did not seem much I could do for them, short of falling over
the side. One of them took my broken ring away and his paper
paid for it to be mended.

Two telegrams arrived. One was from Captain Dodds, the
assistant harbour master of Port Elizabeth, to wish me well, which
I thought was a very kind gesture. I had spoken to him on the
telephone when I had been expecting to go into Port Elizabeth.

The other, less welcome, but not altogether a surprise, was
brought by a *Sunday Times* representative. The telegram said I was
disqualified from the race, subject to confirmation ; the *Sunday Times*
man wondered what I had to say about it. It was a good question :
I answered it as best I could by asking how I could be disqualified
from a race that I had never entered.

Chick returned at about 1400 hours, by which time I had begun
to be aware that the prospect of setting foot on land was a prospect
of ever increasing charm. What in all conscience would it matter if I
jumped across those two feet which were separating me from the
shore? Who was going to care, now that I was in East London,
whether I rocked on its river or strolled in its streets? The whole
situation was one of galloping absurdity. It was *English Rose* and
that mid-ocean ship all over again. The chaps on the jetty were as
far removed as ever from understanding my reasons for remaining
where I was, and I could quite appreciate their difficulty. I turned
my back on temptation and went below.

That evening, Andrew Hutcheson returned with a party of sailing
club men. I still could not step ashore, so on the mountain and
Mahomet principle they came aboard and about a dozen of us had
a party. In the circumstances, it had to be a sit-about-and-talk party,
with two of us sitting on boxes, one on the stairs, one on the chart
table and the rest on the bunks, but it went off very pleasantly.

Chick stayed the night again, but he had to leave next morning
because he was playing in a match in the afternoon. We shook
hands : if everything went all right once my spares had arrived,

we would not be seeing each other again until it was time to start training for the Andes.

'Cherio, boyo', he said. 'Look after yourself.'

'Thanks for all your help, Chick. I wish the bloody stuff would hurry up.'

I was becoming edgy; anxious to get my new servo blade fitted, so that I could end – one way or the other – my uncertainty about what was going to happen when I resumed my fight with the forties. If round two ended in a similar fashion to round one, that would be that. Victory to the elements on a technical knock-out. The first round had made me pretty certain what the outcome would be. All the same, the most certain thing in this life is that you can never be certain of anything, and I wanted to know what was in store.

That afternoon, as a result of a message which Andrew had passed on my behalf, a Catholic priest – Father W. H. Barnes – came to see me. I am not a Catholic, but Maureen is and I have always emerged feeling the better for conversations with priests whom I have called in to help me at times when I have been particularly anxious to put life in perspective. Father Barnes, a fair-haired, fresh-complexioned six-footer, was as helpful as his various predecssors had been. We had a long, long talk about the meaning of everything: religion, apartheid, marriage, children, conscience. He had to leave to conduct a youth discussion group, but he returned in the evening with two books and we began again where we had left off. I was vastly impressed with him, and I asked if he would write to Maureen. He said he would, on condition that I wrote to him when I returned home. I nodded vigorously.

'That's a promise, Father.'

Monday was a long frustrating day. I fitted my remaining spare servo blade so that I would be ready to leave as soon as the ones for which I was waiting arrived. As usual, a freight services representative turned up to say that there had been nothing for me on the afternoon flight from Johannesburg. Andrew telephoned Maureen from his office to tell her what was happening, and he returned with the message that I was to keep my pecker up and that everything was fine in Newcastle.

Tuesday, September 17, turned out to be the day I had been waiting for. Late in the afternoon, a man brought me two servo blades, and other equipment which included extra screws for the self-steering gear, a drill and three more spinners for the Walker's log. Andrew suggested that as it was getting on for dusk I should stay where I was and set off in the morning, but I said I thought I had been playing side-by-side with South Africa for long enough. It was time to go.

Andrew gave me his East London Sailing Club burgee, which I stowed safely away and then – by courtesy of the pilot launch – I was on my way. I was towed the half mile back to the breakwater, where I hoisted sail – and this, after the long days of waiting, was an exhilarating experience in itself. Soon, the bow wave was hissing in the twilight and *Dytiscus* was going nose-up for Australia, as if she were glad to be a boat again instead of a floating doss house. I stood on the deck, with the breeze skipping through my hair, and watched the lights of East London speckling the night astern. I was leaving behind some splendid characters and I wondered if I would ever see them again. Not that this was exactly the time for sentimentatily. Every yard of progress was a yard nearer the answer to the question of what the immediate future held for me. And if *Dytiscus* could not take what was coming, then my coy courtship of East London had all been so much waste of time : I would merely have been postponing my acknowledgment of the inevitable, perhaps only by a matter of days. Because if *Dytiscus* could not take it, that would be the end of the road for the novice in the non-stop. Not that I was a novice any more, of course : you can't travel more than eight thousand miles single-handed without learning something of the ways of sail and sea. And one of the things I had learned beyond doubt was that the sea was not to be trifled with; that it was always ready to transform a slip into a catastrophe; that to confront it ill-equipped was to buy a one-way ticket to disaster. I remembered what Ronald Nierop had told me when he had offered me the boat : 'Go only if you are happy with the design.' Those were words whose pertinence was mutliplied a score of times now that it was the Roaring Forties, instead of the Solent, which were awaiting my going. I also remembered the promise I had made to Maureen under the eyes of my impassive audience on the East London jetty : 'I am not going to do anything foolish . . . ."

I went below and made myself some coffee. Soon, all the answers would be given.

But not, it appeared, just yet : four hours later, I was becalmed, and I stayed becalmed for five hours. I went to bed, leaving my mainsail looking for a breeze.

The breeze came next day, building up gradually to a force six. *Dytiscus* was skipping along, and she went on skipping through the night, until Thursday, September 19, found me well over two hundred miles out of East London and trying conclusions with a storm force ten, with winds of up to fifty-five knots. One moment, the bow was pointing to the heavens, its outline blurred beyond the flying grey mist; the next, it was showing me the way down, pell-mell into a newly-formed valley between monstrous, menacing mountains that were never still for an instant. Stinging spray lashed my face. Salt found my eyes. Curdsy spume flicked off the wave-tops like a hail of confetti at a demon's wedding, showering a million needles from the mountains of hell which towered high above my masthead. I was under storm jib and trailing warps in a bid to slow the yacht, which was beginning to surf. There was nothing else I could do, so I went below and sat down on my bunk. Within minutes, I had cause to be thankful that I had not stayed on deck. The boat was suddenly picked up and slammed on her side with a cacophonous crash. Cupboards burst open. A jerrycan of water gambolled across the floor. Everything that could fly was flying as the saloon windows on the port side lay down in the sea. Convinced by the noise that I had been dismasted, I lurched aloft. The joy with which I discovered that my mast, although horizontal, was still at ninety degrees to the deck, was tempered by the realization that a colossal wall of green water was about to fall on me. I shut my eyes and held on like a limpet as I waited for the crash. Then, when I had emerged from my own Niagara, soaked and spluttering in the screaming wind, I edged my way to the tiller, fought to disconnect the self-steering gear and then set about trying to bring the boat round again, so that she was no longer sideways-on to the blockbusting barrage of water.

After what seemed an age, I won the battle to get her sailing. Then I set the self-steering gear – and immediately realized that the sea had claimed my servo blade again. There was nothing for it but to heave-to while I fitted the first of my two replacement blades in its place.

I again persuaded numbed fingers to undo all the ropes from the tiller to the self-steering gear, so that I could bring the servo gear inboard and take it downstairs. Once below, I fitted the new servo blade, checked the alignment, and put on a new shear wire.

Ninety minutes after the crash that had spelled disaster, I was on my way again. By this time, the wind was gusting force eleven – fifty-six to sixty-three knots – and I was an extremely worried man. The waves were the biggest I had ever seen.

But there was no let-up. Later in the day, *Dytiscus* was picked up and knocked over a second time – this time when I was standing at the cooker. And this time, when everything flew across the saloon, I flew with it, cutting my head when I banged into the locking bar of the speedometer. The seas were absolutely colossal, marching with an implacable fury that gave no hint of growing tired. *Dytiscus* was doing her best, but in such company her best was just not good enough. All day, the terrifying pantomime continued, with the boat tightroping between survival and catastrophe and somehow managing to absorb everything that was coming to her. I was chilled with foreboding. *Blyth, you're barmy!*

Time after time, the boat broached, turning ninety degrees to the waves. Usually, she managed to remain upright. But in the early hours of the following morning, Friday, September 20, she was turned sideways and flattened – all nine tons of her – for the third time. I was in my bunk when it happened, so the flying sequence managed without me. Again I stumbled upstairs to bring the boat round. And when I had done so, I went below again to analyse the situation.

I had twelve thousand miles of the Roaring Forties still to go before I reached Cape Horn, and the two servo blades had broken in the course of a mere five hundred miles. Five hundred miles of actual progress, that is : it was considerably more than that once you allowed for my return journey – but actual progress was what counted, and two blades in five hundred miles represented a totally disproportionate tendency towards trouble.

I had never intended to be in the Roaring Forties in winter, naturally. I was here because I had crashed southwards far more quickly than anyone had exepected me to, and because I had set off, against the advice of my experienced friends, a month earlier than I had originally intended, in hot pursuit of John Ridgway.

The boat broached as readily when I tried steering by tiller
If I went on, anything might happen.
as she did under self-steering gear, which meant an interesting future whichever course I adopted. And even if I managed to avoid breaking either of my two remaining servo blades, I was obviously

in with a chance of collecting a hole in the deck and taking in more of the Indian Ocean than I could possibly feel comfortable with. The beauty of fibreglass boats is that you can mend them fairly easily – but, as the note says with the mending instructions, only when the surface to be mended is clean and dry. And clean, dry surfaces are a bit hard to come by when the sea is vomiting all over you in a raging gale.

Supposing I went on, it would take me three months to reach Australia and be in a position to let Maureen know where I was and how I was. In those three months, people would constantly be asking her if there was any news, and she would have to say that there was not. Then they would say, 'He'll be all right', but what they would think would be *He's had it*. And the trouble was, they could very well be right.

As the rampaging battalions of my raging personal hell continued to crash on the coach roof above my head, it was becoming more apparent by the minute that to go on in these conditions would be to ask too much of Maureen and too much of the boat.

I came into it, too, of course. I make no bones about acknowledging that I was having the fright of my life. Anyone who could claim to come through a screaming waterborne cataclysm like the one that was just the other side of my saloon windows without admitting that fear was having a joy-ride at his expense would be either lacking in imagination or accuracy.

The odd thing is that in such a situation fear does not influence you. When I made my decision, as I then did, to turn about and head for Port Elizabeth, it would probably have been easier for me to decide to carry on. Had I been younger or unmarried, I might have taken the chance and done so, because so many people had given so much time, effort and money to set me on my way – and I had my full share of that vanity which is inborn in all men, the vanity which makes captains go down with their ships for no reason at all. But what sort of time was this for vanity? I looked at Maureen and baby Samantha in the picture in the galley. They were the ones who mattered now. I had no right to sacrifice their future just so that the obituaries could say that Blyth had gone bravely to his untimely end; no right to die just because I was afraid that I might be accused of failure. I had promised Maureen that commonsense would prevail, and that was what commonsense was going to do.

I contacted Port Elizabeth and radioed a telegram to the girl who had trusted me not to do anything stupid when she had agreed to let me go in the first place. Not to do anything stupid, that is, above and beyond the incredibilities of the circumstances which had attended my going – the follow-my-leader system which had ensured my safe emergence from the Hamble, and the innocence of practical navigation which had had me lost in Lyme Bay.

Above all now, I wanted Maureen to come out to South Africa to join me. Then we could sail *Dytiscus* home together and at least salvage something from the ashes of my adventure.

My telegram said : 'Going into Port Elizabeth. Discontinuing voyage. Will you fly out? If answer yes, await further instructions. Commonsense must prevail. Metrobeale.' '

I thanked the radio operator. Then I went on deck and turned about.

* * * * * *

After a few more days of uncertain progress through the storm, I was in Port Elizabeth. There I met a German couple who were proposing to sail their boat to South America, although he could not navigate. As a former non-navigator, I took my hat off to him, and I tried to give him what help I could over a cup of tea and sandwiches aboard their yacht. It was not an altogether successful session, because all his tables were in German and had me beaten from the beginning. Then a young South African couple, friends of the Germans, took me on a quick tour of Port Elizabeth to show me the flood damage which the storm had caused. As I stepped ashore, I felt my conscience give me a short, sharp kick. I dealt with it immediately. *Shut up, it's all over now.*

When I arrived back at the harbour, Alex Eales, a sports writer on the *Eastern Province Herald,* and Ian Barclay-Logie, a businessman, were waiting for me at the quayside. They were both friends of Chick, who had asked them to meet me after I had telephoned to tell him when I expected to reach Port Elizabeth. Alex said that Chick's idea was that I should fly to Johannesburg to join Chick there, so that we could both meet Maureen off the plane. Maureen and I could then spend a few days with Chick and Lisa before we began the voyage home.

Unfortunately, I was hardly dressed for flying. The last three-and-a-half months had not left me in any danger of being mistaken for the pride of Savile Row. So while Alex went to check the time of the plane to Johannesburg, I went with Ian to his home and borrowed one of his suits, a shirt and a tie. His shoes were far too big for me, so we borrowed a pair from a neighbour. Then Alex rang to say that the plane left in thirty-five minutes, so we made a frantic dash to the airport, where Alex arranged for my ticket, using Chick's money.

As the plane soared northwards, I could not help feeling that it was all a bit ridiculous. Within four hours of touching land for the first time, after spending so long uncomfortably at sea doing a maximum of about seven knots except when *Dytiscus* was surfing, I was now speeding luxuriously along in a Boeing 707 at something like six hundred miles per hour. I probably looked like any of the several businessmen who were aboard. The difference was that they could presumably claim ownership of rather more than their socks and underwear.

I fingered Ian Barclay-Logie's tie, hitched the knees of his trousers and shuffled his neighbour's shoes. Well, if it *wasn't* ridiculous, I would have liked to know what it was.

Chick and Lisa were waiting at Johannesburg airport. Forty minutes later, I was at their flat, meeting their children – Jamie, aged three, and Richard, aged six – and telling Chick that yes, I thought a beer was a good idea.

Next morning, the three of us took Jamie – Richard was at school – to the airport to meet Maureen. Chick had a friend in the customs, and he got Maureen through the formalities very quickly. She was a trim little figure in a coffee coloured dress with white accessories, and she looked about her with just a hint of uncertainty until she spotted us in the waiting crowd from about fifteen feet. Then, as realization dawned that the reception party included me, momentary disbelief became the radiant smile that I had not seen for far too long. Until that instant, she had been under the impression that I was waiting for her in Port Elizabeth, and that the responsibility for doing the Johannesburg honours would fall solely on Chick and Lisa.

'Chay! Whatever are *you* doing here?'

The words bubbled with that slight hint of Geordieland which I have always found so attractive in her. I was going to tell her it was a long story, but before I had time she followed through smartly with a bonus issue of even more bewilderment.

'And whose clothes are you wearing?'

'Everybody's', I assured her.

'And how did you get here without a passport?'

It was time, in the interests of diplomacy, to call a halt.

'That', I said firmly, 'is my secret.'

I squeezed her waist with one arm, indicated Chick with the other.

'Chick says we are to stay for a day or two before we push off home.'

Chick grinned.

'If you two don't finish your crosstalk act, your holiday will be over before it's started.'

* * * * * *

Our day or two with Chick and Lisa turned into a fortnight. Chick and I spent a lot of the time strengthening the foundations of the plan we had hatched aboard *Dytiscus*. We made frequent visits to the library, garnering every factor we could about the problems which were likely to be ours up the Andes and down the Amazon.

It was while Chick and I were out on our first reconnaissance that Lisa told Maureen what we had in mind. Lisa was not exactly keen on the idea at that stage, and when we returned I did not have to ask for footnotes to realize that Maureen could hardly be described as inspired by it. The four of us repeatedly spent hours talking it out, sounding the possibilities, recognizing the hazards. Towards the end of our stay, Lisa seemed to be coming round to realizing that there would be no question of our undertaking it other than in a state of the most complete preparedness it was possible to achieve; no question, for example, of our setting forth with a ninepenny tin of sticking plaster and thinking we were medically equipped. Maureen knew this already, of course: she knew me, and she knew the detailed planning which had gone into my associations with *English Rose* and *Dytiscus*. What was bothering her was that she thought it was too soon to begin talking about another adventure.

Chick and I, on the other hand, were quite prepared to talk from dawn to dusk. For my part, I knew that the planning of any adventure was far more enjoyable than the adventure itself and it seemed a shame to miss the planning now that Chick and I had the chance. Another ex-paratrooper, Butch Buchan, whom we had

Maureen in the Roaring Forties.

An escort of porpoises.

Maureen keeps her safety harness clipped on.

Dytiscus is a 30 foot long resin-glass sloop of the Kingfisher class.

known in the regiment and who was now on his way to join the Rhodesian Special Air Service, came in on our discussions with advice based on his service with the Special Air Service in Malaya and Borneo.

But if I did not agree that it was too soon to begin talking about another adventure, I could see that it was too soon to commit myself finally to one. Chick agreed that it was something we ought to think about for a little while longer, and Lisa, on whom Maureen had been working with some diligence, also saw the sense in advancing with caution.

At the end of our holiday, our friends came with us to the airport to see us off on our flight to Port Elizabeth. When we said our goodbyes, the plan was still in the air. A few minutes later, we were in the air, too.

10

Sea for Two

Maureen Blyth : October 8 – October 30

DYTISCUS III looked so spruce, sitting at her mooring with the water chuckling and slupping between her bright red hull and the jetty. Nobody who did not know would have suspected the sort of troubles she had had to put up with since she and Chay had set off down the Hamble exactly four months ago to the day. She seemed such a proud, pert boat as she gleamed in the warm South African sunshine, and I was eager for the moment when I could step aboard and become a part of her story – the story which I had had to follow until now at an ever-increasing distance, with only my imagination and my dreams to supplement the half-dozen letters and rather more telegrams which Chay had sent me.

She was proud, and I was proud, too. Proud of the way *Dytiscus* had proved herself strong enough to put up with the Roaring Forties, even though the conditions had made her broach so many times.

And proud of this crazy joker of a husband of mine, who had insisted on attempting the impossible, and who could not be blamed for the fact that he had not achieved it. This had been the first time that one of his adventures had depended on a complex piece of equipment, and that piece of equipment was the thing that had stopped him. In his Arctic and desert survival courses, his long-distance canoe races and his Atlantic row, he had had to depend on himself and he had won through every time. He had not said much about the premature end to his circumnavigation, and I was pretty sure that in his own mind he had written himself down as a failure, but that was not the way I saw it. Without being able to sail or navigate, he had set off to go round the world in the wrong type of boat, and it had taken the Roaring Forties in winter to stop him. I was impatient to get the customs and other formalities behind us. I wanted to see for myself the way this husband of mine tackled the winds and the sea.

It's funny, how quickly ideas are changed by circumstances. I fairly skipped aboard, clutching the bottle of wine which we had bought in Port Elizabeth to drink with our first dinner at sea and ready to start learning to be the crew of Skipper Blyth. Already, he had begun calling me Number One. There was a flutter of butterflies in my tummy as Chay cast off and began to do something or other with the sails. I stood in the cockpit as we got under way, and I could not help thinking that the man in charge looked vastly more at home with his canvas than he had done on June 8, when he was playing follow-my-leader behind Neville Wood, doing exactly what Neville did and hoping that nobody would suspect a thing.

As I watched him now, with the breeze in my hair and the boat beginning to respond to the slight swell of the water, I felt a tingle of excitement; a bubbling awareness of an approaching adventure which I had never dreamed would come my way until the arrival of Chay's cable about a fortnight ago.

But, as I say, circumstances have a way of altering your approach to a situation – and it gradually began to dawn on me that circumstances were changing as we slipped beyond the harbour bar at 5.15 p.m. South African time, radioing our destination to the harbour master as we did so. The white-shirted operator waved as we passed him goose-winged – that is, with the mainsail on one side and the genoa on the other. And now we were no longer enclosed reassuring in the womb of Port Elizabeth harbour : we were outside and at sea – born, you might say, to the realities of ocean-going in a thirty-foot yacht.

I looked back over the stern at the safety we were leaving behind – into the harbour, where about two dozen small sailing and cruising craft were bobbing among five merchant vessels. The two British ships among them had brought a lump to my throat by acknowledging our red ensign with a 'Bon voyage' signal before we had passed the breakwater. Now, on our starboard beam was a vast stretch of sand, guarded by some rocky outcrops and backed by a mixture of buildings.

Then I brought my gaze to my immediate surroundings – to this little red boat, which suddenly seemed so ridiculously small out here on this serene and thoughtful sea – and I realized that my tingle of excitement was giving way to plain, straightforward horror and dismay. *Dytiscus,* who had seemed so confident and alert in the harbour, had become a frail, uncertain little craft on this expanse of open ocean.

Already, I realized in sudden panic, the rigging was groaning. The boat itself was creaking in all sorts of strange places, as if it were trying to decide just which of those places ought to split apart first. And I was proposing to sail eight thousand miles home in *this?* I must be as mad as my husband!

All I could do was resolve to get used to it just as soon as I could – and try not to be seasick. I wanted to be a good sailor and not get in Chay's way more than was absolutely necessary until I got into the run of things. I tried hard, too, not to do anything stupid – but this was quite difficult. Every time a wave hit *Dytiscus* when I was down below and had not seen it coming, it startled me into exclaiming, 'What was that?' For the first few times, Chay told me; after, that he let me work it out for myself. Every couple of minutes, after I had turned my attentions to preparing a meal, I was being thrown about the saloon. I had yet to learn I must always hold on or be ready to grab for support, and I was grateful that the gimbled cooker did not throw things after me. I did my best to resist remarking how rough the sea was, but in the end I had to. I wished I hadn't, though : Chay said it was not at all rough. I felt the best thing I could do was to make myself useful in a way that I knew by heart : so while Chay scrubbed the deck down and checked all the gear, I had a washday – and got most of the things dry by hanging them on the guard rail and lying them on the coach roof. By this time, I had put our wine bottle safely away in the forward compartment : we had decided to open it at the Equator, rather than at dinner in the first flush of together-ness. And the Equator, we hoped, would be beneath us about November 12.

By that time, if I did not prove too silly, I might know a little more about the mysteries of seamanship with which I was now surrounded for the first time in my life. Chay made an early start on my education by showing me how to read the compass and work out the radio on the 2182 emergency frequency during our second day out. I had a feeling he would have to tell me again, but it was a beginning.

The next day, I began to understand why Chay had not thought the sea was rough before. All day, the wind built up until Chay said it was force nine. I began to realise just what he and John had meant when they said that the waves were as big as houses during their Atlantic crossing. They came crashing over the saloon roof and filling up the cockpit, and *Dytiscus* went ploughing on at a terrifying six knots. I was petrified and absolutely certain that I was going to be sick, and I went into what Chay started calling my ostrich act – lying on my bunk and curling up small with my head inside my sleeping bag, where I slept fitfully and prayed frantically. I decided that I really must be mad : don't they say that if you live long enough with a person, you grow like him?

My husband, meanwhile, got drenched when he went outside to empty the rubbish pail without putting his coat on. Typical Chay!

The gale went on all the next day until about five o'clock. I had awakened to the most dreadful seas : they were like giant jaws, just open and waiting. The waves battered at us from all directions. I simply could not believe the size of them. But Chay was an absolute darling. He went out of his way to give me anything I wanted, and I was sure he knew how miserable I felt – although I was doing my best to keep my troubles to myself. Oddly, it was not until things had died down a little that I was sick.

Then, in the evening, I sat in the cockpit before supper and told myself that there was no need to be frightened of the waves which were still heaving at *Dytiscus* like huge mountains while we lurched about in the valley. I wrote in my log : 'Any single one of those waves, whether large or small, could rip us to pieces if God so wished. If He wants us to get home safely, He will take us home safely.' And, somehow, I was sure that this was what God did want : He wanted us to get back home to little Samantha Fiona, who was with my mother in Newcastle-upon-Tyne. Our target was to be home by Christmas – but whether we achieved it on time or not, I felt certain that we would be spared to see home again sometime or other.

My belief was strengthened when the weather mended its manners and gave us two days of sunshine. I had a good wash, changed all my clothes, sunbathed on the saloon roof. Lunch in the cockpit was tomatoes, cheese and onions with cream crackers, followed by fresh oranges. As we ate, we talked – mostly about S.F., whom Chay was calling Number Two. It had not been easy for me to choose between coming out to Chay or staying with Samantha, but I felt that Chay needed me most, after being at sea for more than three months and then finding that he had to call the circumnavigation off because of all the broaching. All the same, when we played two games of ludo in the afternoon and he won both of them, I did rather let rip at him. I was livid!

I was not all that pleased, either, when a lesson in sail-hoisting resulted in my banging my head on the spinnaker boom. But I put it down to the price of my education, and I managed to raise and lower the ghosting genoa twice on my own after Chay had taken me through the operation once.

Somehow or other, though, I kept getting in the way when he was trying to take his noon sight – but he was very patient, and he duly reported that we were now heading towards Cape Agulhas, the southern tip of South Africa. What I was looking forward to was turning right at Cape Town, which Chay said was about a hundred and eighty miles ahead : I wanted to send a cable to Mummy when we got there, because I knew she would be worried about us.

Meanwhile, I was beginning to enjoy my various duties as Number One, although they were accompanied by the arrival of a rash of heat lumps all over me, from my neck to my waist. The only bit of complaining I did was when Chay shaved for the first time in six days : I had grown to like seeing him behind a beard.

I am afraid, however, that in these early days it was all too easy for me to have a change of heart. And when another gale started in the night of October 13, I changed just as quickly as the weather. Being sick before dawn helped to persuade me that I never wanted to see another boat again. Then Chay got me a drink at 1.30 p.m., and he frightened me to death by suddenly giving a terrific shout as he looked out of the saloon window.

'Hell! There's a ship coming straight for us!'

I scrambled out of bed and panicked about, looking for the flares while he tried to put his coat on and switch the radio to the emergency frequency all in one movement. It was complete chaos. Chay went into the cockpit, waving frantically as the ship kept on coming. It got to within two hundred yards of us, by which time I had completely forgotten my seasickness because that was quite close enough for two ships in a gale. Then it turned, and Chay shouted again.

'It's a Russian! Give me the camera, quick!'

He took some pictures, then the ship did a ninety-degree turn and shot away from us : I am sure the camera frightened it away, but Chay said it was probably just curious about us and was making sure we were not in trouble. He wondered if the Russians were there because the American Apollo spacecraft was due for splashdown.

'Tell you one thing, Number One', he said, as we stood and watched the ship's departure. 'We'll have to work out some emergency drills so that in future we don't get in each other's way.'

'Aye, aye, Skipper', I said.

Well, you have to humour these men, don't you?

We spent most of that day hove to, because the gale was preventing us from making any progress west. The next day was no better, and I was worse : sick and miserable and wondering whatever had made me think I could be a sailor. Somehow, nothing seemed to affect Chay – and seeing him scrambling about the lurching boat. making himself useful in all directions, only made me feel more depressed than ever over my own inability to cope. I was tired of being buffetted and thrown about, and my tummy was tied in knots. I was beginning to believe we would never get past Cape Agulhas, let alone turn right at Cape Town. In my mind, the most wonderful thing in the world was beginning to be an armchair – a big, solid armchair that was soft and comfortable and actually stayed still for three seconds on end, unlike this leaping boat which had become my home because I had a wonderful, crazy husband and because I was obviously as mad as he was. I sat in the cockpit, being drenched by the waves and feeling frozen to the marrow, and I told myself that this was no place for the mother of a fifteen-month-old infant to be in.

Chay developed a small boil on his nose and enlisted me as its nursemaid. I could not think what had caused it : certainly not lack of food, because the man simply never stopped eating. Never! Nothing was wasted when Chay was about. So I nursed his nose and gave him lots of sympathy, because that is what he likes whenever there is anything the matter with him. But it was not only his nose that was worrying him, as he confided while I was surveying the excresccence and asking him if he would prefer a split or a tourniquet.

'I shall be glad when we are out of the shipping lanes', he said. 'I don't like this business of never knowing when we are going to meet something. You go all day without seeing one, but as soon as it's dark they seem to be all round you, wherever you look.'

He was right. Every day, we seemed to have the ocean to ourselves; every night, we were apparently surrounded by ships. The unpleasant thing was that we could not judge how far away they were, because all we had to go on was their lights, which looked like clusters of fireflies. A South African frigate – at least, that's what Chay said it was – came across to us out of the gloom and somebody on board shouted at us through a loud hailer. We could not make out what he was saying, but it seemed to be something about oil rig. Chay altered course, and the ship left us – apparently satisfied that we would not now be running into the rig.

The gale, however, showed no sign of leaving us, and water was coming in everywhere. The floor of the saloon was permanently awash under about two inches, in spite of our persistent baling out operations. Our clothes were damp because there had been no opportunity to dry the m out. Home comforts had never seemed so important.

How I longed for a roaring fire to sit by and a chunky crust of farmhouse loaf, thickly spread with butter and smothered with blackcurrant jam! And here I was, stuck in an unsympathetic sea and likely to remain stuck for at least another two months. Even some of the home comforts with which we had tried to provide ourselves had failed to live up to expectations : the fresh apples which we had gleefully bought in Port Elizabeth were overtaken by old age before we had worked our way through them, and we had to throw a bag of them overboard. They had been separately wrapped, too. All I now needed, I felt, was for my hot water bottle to spring a leak.

But at least, by Saturday, October 19, we were at last past the Cape of Good Hope, and I knew exactly why its other name is the Cape of Storms. It had taken us eleven days, instead of the six or seven we had expected – which was the time we had told Mummy she would have to wait before we could send her a cable. Getting the cable off was a load off my conscience, because I knew she would be worried stiff. I took a thankful look at Table Mountain, which was on our starboard quarter – I think – twenty or thirty miles away. We also had a link call to Chick and Lisa, in Johannesburg. They came through as clear as a bell. It was wonderful to hear them and to realize that perhaps we were not completely cut off from life after all. The call and the cable made me feel a lot better, although the seas went on raging. Chay seemed to notice a change in me.

'Number One', he said 'you brighten the place up.'

He admired my Mia Farrow haircut, which I had adopted for purely practical reasons, because it needed very little attention to keep it tidy. He even went out of his way to catch a bucketful of rainwater so that I could wash it – and I kicked it over and lost the lot. I was furious – not so much at losing my hairwash as because it was a little kindness which Chay had thought of without my having had to ask him.

As we began to head north-west before a southerly wind, the boat started to behave in such an unusual way that even I noticed that something seemed to be different. Chay explained that we were yawing all over the place, although it was only a force seven wind.

'This is the sort of thing I am talking about when I say the boat won't run well under self-steering gear', he said. 'You wait until we get a really good blow behind us!'

I did not have long to wait before I found out. That very night, the winds and the sea mounted a major attack from astern. The boat kept going over on her side, and there would be a noise like thunder and a terrible battle as she struggled to come upright again. This, I thought, must be what had been happening in the roaring forties, when the self-steering gear kept breaking. The only difference was that in the Roaring Forties the seas would have been much larger.

During the evening, a rogue wave hit us with a terrific smack. It almost knocked us horizontal, and the tape recorder, clock, batteries and a host of other things went flying across the saloon. Chay dashed on deck and found that one stanchion had been bent over to about forty-five degrees and the rear guard rail had been buckled and pushed right through the fibre glass of the aft cabin, so that water was pouring in through two holes.

Chay fixed some rubber across as a temporary measure, while the sea kept on flying over his back. He said that when things quietened down he would do one of his fibre-glassing jobs on it. There did not seem to be any prospect of this happening for some time. The elements just went on throwing everything at us. Chay went into the cockpit to put a warp over when all of a sudden an enormous wave hit us. I looked out of the saloon and there he was, sitting with an absolutely disgusted expression on his face, up to his knees in water and using words that dictionaries have never thought of.

The seas were quite fantastic, engulfing the yacht on all sides. We were on deck when another wave came over the stern – and over us. We were drenched, and I did not really feel less drenchd when Chay took the trouble to explain that we had just been pooped.

Then we found that the radio telephone was out of action when Chay tried to contact Cape Town Radio. This meant that we had no Mayday and we could not let anybody know where we were. Chay said he would strip it down on the first fine day we had. What with this and the fibre-glassing, I could see he was going to be busy. I tried to help. Would he *have* to strip down? Couldn't it, perhaps, be the battery?

'Nothing wrong with the battery, that's for sure. All the batteries were charged in Port Elizabeth. Don't worry – I'll strip it down.'

Further discussion was pointless. The master had spoken.

That night, about two hours after disaster had struck the aft cabin, there was another tremendous crash up on deck, interrupting the cup of tea which we were having in the saloon. We scrambled out into the darkness, shining a torch and dreading what it would reveal.

It turned out that one of the forward bottle screws had parted, and the forestay was hanging like a dead snake. Only the sail hanks were preventing it from swaying all over the place and becoming very dangerous.

Chay told me to go back inside while he fixed it, but a minute later he was calling me again.

'You'll have to come, Maureen : my mouth isn't big enough to hold the torch.'

'Who do you think you're kidding?'

I shouted the question in competition with the force nine gale and the crash of the foaming water which was swilling without interruption across the deck. Still, if the master wanted me I had better go. Forward, little wife and mother! With my safety harness firmly secured to the lifeline, which ran the length of the boat. I crawled towards where he was sitting with his back to the pulpit and his legs braced against a side stanchion. Then, jamming myself beside him in the darkness, I went into my Statue of Liberty act to enable Chay to see what he was doing. It was quite an experience. The waves kept pounding over us, and every few minutes it was necessary to hang on for dear life or else be swept overboard. Altogether, we were there for two hours. By this time, I was about

stupefied with the cold. Above the frightening racket, I shouted:
'If this is what you mean by survival, you can keep it!' And what
did the man do? He *grinned!*

But then, with the job done and Chay's watch saying it was
2.30 a.m., it was time to get back below. I eased myself up cautiously
and began a sort of half-crawl towards the cockpit, with Chay just
behind me.

Another wave hit us, and in the midst of its thunder I heard
Chay yell: 'Hang on! For God's sake, hang on!' Then I was sent
spread-eagling across the deck until I ended up holding the bar
on the coach roof while my feet hung over the port side. For a
moment, I just hung there, petrified, before I scrambled to safety.
It frightened Chay, too, I could tell. Moments like that are supposed
to bring a husband and wife closer together — but I felt I would
prefer to do my best to struggle on without their assistance.

One way and another, it was the sort of night that was a world
away from the life I had been leading until two weeks previously.
It was a night which I simply could not have imagined if I had
stayed at home and left Chay to bring the boat back on his own.
All the crashing horror of it was now a part of me in a way it
could never have been if I had had to rely on Chay's account of it
and my own imagination. And in a strange way I was glad to have
been able to share it — now that it was all over — with this wandering
husband of mine. It had somehow admitted me to a part of him of
which I had always been aware but which had until now always
been hidden behind a door I could not open. I was beginning to see
that there can be a sort of horrid fascination about the power of
nature, even though there is nothing very appealing about the
times when you feel that nature is running a personal vendetta
against you and there seems nothing that you can do but sit and
take what is coming. In the past, when Chay had outlined his hopes
for various adventures, I had listened without really understanding.
But now I was beginning to find his wavelength . . . .

The difference between us was that Chay remained so calm
when disaster struck, whereas I promptly went like jelly. I was
always aware that he had an inner strength on which he seemed
able to call whenever it was needed. I tried to find strength in
prayer. I prayed as I had never prayed before.

Next day, the seas had gone down considerably, and I was sure
my prayers had had something to do with it. Like Chay, I am

convinced that many things which people put down as coincidence
are not coincidence at all.

The trouble was, the seas went on going down until they had
gone down too far and the winds had gone with them. We had moved
from gale to calm : it seemed I had prayed too hard! But I was not
going to grumble too soon. It was heaven to feel the boat steady
beneath me and to see the sun above me, and to be warm and
clean and dry, which was how I felt by the time I had washed my
hair, had a bath in the cockpit, and settled down to a sunbathe on
the saloon roof. I caught up with all our washing and got it all dry
on the guard rails, and Chay did his fibre-glassing on the aft cabin
and began charging the batteries. I ran into trouble when I climbed
into the cockpit just as Chay had decided to hoist the mainsail.
The boom hit me in the face and gave me an impressive bump
under my left eye. I cried like a baby. What a sailor!

I sought consolation in my birthday cake, which we had got
out of its tin a little while earlier. We demolished two-thirds of
it and it was gorgeous. Betty Ridley had made it for Chay to
celebrate September 26, but the South African interlude had upset
that bit of planning and we were only now, nearly a month later,
realizing what we had been missing.

For dinner, I made a curry with a tin of stewing steak. We chased
it down with whisky. Marvellous!

With the calms, however, there is always the danger of boredom
and frustration. Day followed day, and our progress was minimal.
Sixty miles, fifty miles, sixty-five miles. We were getting virtually
nowhere, and Chay was having no luck with his efforts as a radio
mechanic, which did not altogether please him. We decided we had
better call on St Helena and holler for a technician if it was a good
day when we were within striking distance : Chay said that if it was
not a good day he would not go anywhere near it. I am not sure
why, but it sounded rather ominous : perhaps because he had tackled
Tristan da Cunha in a high wind and without the help of detailed
charts. Still, we were a long way from St Helena at the moment –
something like fifteen hundred miles – so the problem was not going
to arise for some time. All the same, I got settled down to write a
letter to Mummy, ready for posting when we got there. I didn't tell
her about my face, which was black and blue from my argument
with the boom.

Time was hanging heavy, and although I did not smoke at all

in the first six days of the trip I was now more than making up
for it. Certainly, this was nothing like home, where there was
young S.F. to keep me running round from morning to night,
quite apart from the routine household chores. A niggling touch of
toothache did not help much – but I met that with a resolve that
I was not going to let my husband dabble in dentistry on my
account, even if it meant my keeping it for three months. And three
months, at the present rate of progress, did not seem at all an
unlikely estimate.

The boat was creaking and wheezing like an old man trying to
climb a hill. My eyes began to feel tired because of all the reading
and writing I was doing in the absence of any diversions. Chay said
we ought to be at St Helena in about ten days, in spite of the
barnacles which were helping to slow us down. Boredom brought
out a tin of crab from the forward compartment : we wanted something exciting for lunch, so we tossed up between lobster and crab,
and crab lost. And we found a tin of partridge, which we earmarked
for Equator day with our bottle of wine. We also dug out the
Christmas cake, two months early, to go with our afternoon drink,
and we passed a gentle fifteen minutes by altering all our clocks
and watches from South African time to Greenwich Mean time.
We played some more ludo, with quite ridiculous intensity. And
I gave Chay an afternoon lecture on parenthood which did not
seem to have an enormous affect on him. I was prompted by the
feeling of being between the devil and the deep blue sea – wanting
him to settle down so that we could have a normal family life
with little S.F., yet also wanting him to fulfil his ambitions so that
his adventurous streak would die naturally. So I talked and I talked
and I talked, and Chay did his best to pretend that he found the
whole thing fascinating. Unfortunately, he was not quite able to
keep his eyelids from drooping.

Every day was odd job day. The Skipper, with his own unfailing
charm, gave me the worst job of the lot.

'I think we'd better have the winches greased, Number One . . . .'

From the way he spoke, it was perfectly obvious that if the
winches were going to wait for the boss man they were going to
wait until they had more or less locked solid.

I looked daggers ; saw without surprise that he did not seem to
be noticing as he gave me my briefing; and reached for the grease
can. Strangely, once I was up to my elbows in the filthy stuff, the

whole unbecoming exercise seemed to be somehow less horrid. I actually began to enjoy it.

One of my other jobs was to knit myself another hat. I had the feeling that once we reached the North Atlantic, I would be glad of two hats, supposing I got as far as leaving the saloon. Supposing, also, that we ever reached the North Atlantic. Chay said we were twelve hundred miles from St Helena. What I said was quite unladylike, but it seemed to help my knitting needles along.

Sunday, October 27, put a temporary end to the fine weather. The seas became angry again, coming at us with foamy fangs and cavernous mouths which were plainly ready to swallow us at any time – but at least they enabled us to cover a hundred and five miles, which was something to shout about, and they gave me the chance to help Chay to boom out the sails a couple of times.

This was a great day in another respect as well : the radio came back into operation. It was a great relief to know that we had contact with the outside world again after a whole week of silence. It was a great relief, too, to know that I had such a diligent, mechanically-minded husband, who had been able to work his way through such a maze of tiny wires and plugs until the great moment when he could pronounce upon the exact trouble. He should have been a professor of physics. *The battery was flat!*

'Would you believe it?' he said. 'The battery's flat.'

'I would believe it', I said. 'Any time.'

But I am a good wife : I said it to myself.

The days began to romp past. It is amazing what a difference it makes when you feel you are actually getting somewhere. Three successive days produced an average distance of a hundred and twenty-seven miles. We shot along with three sails up, and I began to forget my doubts about being home in time for Christmas. Chay put our position at 24° 20′ South, 6° 10′ East, and he was as pleased as Punch. 'It's pretty good, Number One. Considering the winds haven't been above force three and we are weighed down by about a billion barnacles.'

On the strength of this change in our fortunes, which suddenly made Christmas with Samantha seem a possibility again, we opened the Burns' Night and Easter parcels. The Easter pack contained a tin of chicken and some Dewar's, which we demolished at dinner after the afternoon had seen us making a preliminary inroad into the chocolate eggs. But we decided to keep for another occasion the Burns' Night haggis – which was accompanied by a card containing the Toast to the Haggis and was a gift from Chay's niece, Margaret, and her husband, Tony Marshall. Even the fact that we had progressed to another chart did not seem to warrant our going the whole hog all in one go.

We sent another cable home, via Walvis Bay Radio : 'Progress good. All is well. Next report Azores. Prayers work miracles. M.C.'

A day later, we were virtually becalmed, and listening again to the repertoire of becalmed noises which *Dytiscus* did so well : the creaking in the rigging, the slightest movement of the stores, the water slupping about beneath the cabin floor.

It went on for four days, each of which meant a hundred miles lost – despite the diligence with which we set about the sails to try to harvest every breath of wind.

Christmas with Samantha? Never.

II

St. Helena

*A*NY sailing day which puts only twenty miles under your belt, as these last few days had got into the way of doing, is a day for talking. A day for tinned ham and water biscuits on the saloon roof, washed down in the sunshine with orange juice or slept off in the shade of lifeless sails. A day for turning to the hard blue sky in search of a hint of a breeze to come; for seeking hope in barely heaving water; and always, between times, for talking.

Number One and I talked our way through breakfast, lunch and dinner; through hot chocolate and coffee in the moonlight; out of October and into November. All the time, the sea listened with a gentle chuckle beneath the bobbing bow as a man and woman, married almost six years, talked their way towards a new awareness of each other. Plans, fears, prejudice, love, the past, the present, the unknown, God, yesterday, dreams, Samantha – they came tumbling in their turn to take their place beneath the microscope which we were holding up to the world and to ourselves.

If we had been at home and doing nothing, none of this would have happened. But on this timeless sea, brittle-bright beneath the understanding heavens, its happening was inevitable. This was our world. *We* were our world, its masters, its total population; its only wrong-righters, its only wrong-doers; and our world was bewilderingly beset by an awareness of our total insignificance, our utter unworthiness, our resolves. Memories.

We exchanged childhoods. We talked of things which had never consciously been kept secret from each other but which somehow had been. Maureen spoke of the time she broke her leg, playing basketball at school. When she was allowed up, but with the plaster still in place, all her girl friends visited her and wrote their names on it. This was fine for a time, but soon the charm wore off and Maureen did her best to cut the cast away – which qualified her for

144

the most impressive roistering her mother could conjure up. Mother was a district nurse at the time and prone to have a feeling for such matters. And I remembered my schoolboy swimming days as a junior member of the Hawick Amateur Swimming Association. We would travel by coach on Saturdays, for meetings in Edinburgh, Carlisle, Newcastle, and all the border area, singing our heads off as we went. I used to try to beat Frank Scott, who was a particular friend at school and who helped Maureen with the work at Ropelaw- shiel before she flew out to Johannesburg. Sometimes, at backstroke, I did beat him; at free style, I had not a hope.

The days passed.

Inexorably, wondrously, nature was grinding us down; fusing us, it seemed, into a single person fired with a consoling, purposeful purity of intent. For this is nature's way. This is the wonder of a loneliness that is shared with the person to whom you are closest. It becomes remarkably easy to feel that you aer the ones with the message which will make a better world, if only the world will listen when you get back and begin spelling it out.

The trouble is, as I already knew, when you get back among the mini-skirts and the four-letter words, the message goes muzzy on you. Within a week, you are back to square one.

'Damn the weather!' I said, getting back to square one without the formality of finding land. This was the sixth day of winds so light as to be virtually weightless, and the absence of exercise was making me feel frustrated and overfed. I did not really mind the overfeeding bit, of course. When Number One whistled me below and uncorked a lunch of ham, potatoes and peas, I was absolutely enchanted. It was the sort of moment that made me feel that single- handed sailing could be considered to have its drawbacks. I contem- plated this splendid spread and went positively beatific on her, pouring forth praise like a well-planned evensong and latching dedicatedly on to a knife and fork. I could teach Maureen nothing about getting the best out of the galley, as I acknowledged while doing justice to her latest offering. And soon, it occurred to me, I was not going to be able to teach her anything about getting the best out of the yacht.

Practically every day, I was introducing her to one or other of sailing's secrets, which I had prised out of *Dytiscus* during my nine-thousand-mile graduation into experience from the Hamble to the Indian Ocean. And practically every day, she was cottoning on to the essence of the exercise with remarkable rapidity. I would throw her one bit of know-how after another, and by and large they seemed to stick with her as firmly as the barnacles were sticking with the boat. I had already taught her to hoist the sails and work the radio, how to use the sextant and how to splice. Now we moved on to discuss the compass and the problems of its deviation and variation. As usual, I became aware that the beauty of teaching Maureen was that she picked things up so quickly; as usual, I could not help marvelling at the fact of my being the teacher.

'It's quite funny, the very idea of my being able to teach anybody anything about navigation', I said, as we pored over a chart and got to work on some imaginary sights. 'Up to about August, it was all black magic to me.'

'You don't fool me', she said. 'It still *is* black magic to you. It's just that somebody up there is on your side.'

Pausing only to quell that suggestion of mutiny by applying the palm of my hand to the trouser seat which was tightly stretched as Number One stood bending over the problem I had set her, I said:

'The point is, I have discovered you don't have to be brilliant to be able to navigate. As long as you can add and subtract without making a mistake, and follow the crib properly, it's not impossible.'

Maureen rubbed a rueful half-square-foot of trouser.

'You're a horror – but I suppose you're right. After all, if brilliance came into it, you would still be going round the Isle of Wight. *Don't you dare!*'

She pivoted before I could move and effectively protected the target area by sitting on it. I grinned down at her.

'Well swivelled! No, seriously, though. I think most people are put off because the people who do not know how to navigate talk about things like azimuth, or the sun's lower limb, or assumed longitude and latitude. But there's really nothing much to it.'

'Come off it, Chay! There's got to be *something* to it.'

'Well, I'll tell you this: if you can't navigate as well as sail by the time we get home, I'll drop you overboard just as soon as we arrive. Half the battle is being interested in learning – and you certainly seem to be that.'

'Well, yes, I am. All the same . . . .'

'Listen Maureen: you will be able to do it standing on your head. And I'll tell you something else: I think you are going to know enough about sailing before you are very much older for you to enter the 1972 single-handed transatlantic race.'

'What!'

The word exploded in a crackle of bight-eyed disbelief. She shook her head slowly, as if savouring the incredibility of it all. Then :

'You must be joking! How on earth could I do that? It's too silly for words.' '

'It's nothing of the sort, Maureen. There will probably be at least two women entering in any case, and I certainly want to have a crack at it. It would be terrific, competing against each other – and by 1972 you could certainly be good enough to try it.'

'Chay, I could not possibly! You're crazy! It's just not the sort of thing that a young mother is expected to do. Anyway, who on earth would lend me a boat?' '

I grinned a bit more.

'That's my girl! Now you're talking.'

'I'm doing nothing of the sort. You're just teasing.'

Perhaps I was just a clown. All the same, as I watched her booming out the ghosting genoa unaided later that day, I told myself that even a clown can have flashes of inspiration. I was certain I had not been talking through my hat. Maureen, I knew, would one day be able to outwit the Atlantic. That's the sort of girl she is.

The calms stayed with us. Maureen caught up on some sailing jargon like leeches and hanks, boom crutch and bowline, clove hitch and cleats. Part of her education was coming by way of Sir Francis Chichester's book, *The Lonely Sea and the Sky*, as she sunbathed on the saloon roof. It ceased to come, alas, the day the book slipped from her grasp and fell overboard, in a temperature of 98°F. in the shade. And I managed to lose our only good eating knife in the same way, which meant that we would have to take turns for the rest of the voyage with the camping knife which I had already adopted at mealtimes.

I also sabotaged a ludo game by inadvertently dropping the die down the bilge – through a hole in the saloon floor which would have been filled by a table leg if I had not dispensed with the table in the interests of space before leaving the Hamble – when Maureen was in a winning position. And I went fishing and caught the boat somewhere unbudgeable beneath the waterline. We found a crack in the servo box which promised trouble for the future; we heard that Nixon had become President of the United States; Maureen used my head to prove that she had no claims to be considered as one of Britain's brightest barbers.

And eventually, on the morning of Friday, November 8, we were able to look upon St Helena. Through the binoculars, it looked like any other piece of volcanic rock jutting out of the sea, with the mist like a necklace ringing the mountains which seemed to be trying to reach for the sky. We had hoped to be there by 1000 hours, but what little wind there was dropped when we were about two miles from the open bay of the harbour and one mile from the precipitous cliffs which had to be passed before we reached the safety of that bay. I had visions of our being caught by the current and taken helplessly into a rocky reception in several hundred feet of water. I sighed one of my thankful ones when the breeze returned, although it was from a different direction, and we eventually got within half a mile of the harbour by dint of insistent tacking. Then, again, we were becalmed. It was 1730 hours—time, we felt, to try to attract somebody's attention. We hoisted the M.I.K. flags ('report me to Lloyds') and the yellow Q flag ('Health authorities, please come aboard – we are free from disease') together, thinking that if such a combination did not bring some response, nothing would, It did not.

We also failed to rouse anybody with the radio, and even when we began hoisting and lowering the four flags in rapid succession, St Helena just sat there and let us get on with it. We felt quite remarkably unwanted, and when a whisper of a breeze returned we decided the best thing to do would be to creep away again and spend the night a little further away from those cliffs. Even then, there was a frustration before we managed it : while we were manoeuvring, we managed to rip the genoa, which meant that once we had reached our overnight station, two miles offshore, a quick repair job was called for. First you tack, then you sew : ask any good dressmaker.

We were up and about at 0500 hours next day, and four hours later we reached the nearest end of the bay. We came within seventy-five yards of the cliffs and there was not a breath of wind, but the sea swelled against the sides of the boat in a succession of alarming crashes. There was an obvious danger that it would smash us against the rocks in retribution for our presumption in approaching without the insurance of an engine. A fisherman who rasped within hailing distance in a small dinghy with an outboard engine struck us as being the most beautiful sight in the world. I gave him a shout.

'Hey! Do you think you can give us a tow in, please?'

He turned his head but he did not reply for a moment. Thinking he had not caught what I had said, I was about to shout again when he came out with his answer.

'Sorry – I haven't got a licence.'

'You *what!*'

Here were Maureen and I in danger of losing somebody else's boat, and all that was worrying our potential saviour was a licence shortage. By this time, we were a mere fifty yards from the cliffs and we were edging closer every moment.

'Look', I shouted. 'You can see what is happening. We're being pushed towards these cliffs and we can't do anything about it. All you've got to do is tow us to a mooring.'

I had the feeling I was wasting my time: the other half of the act simply began shrugging his shoulders and spreading out his hands, palms upwards, in a flurry of unhelpful sympathy.

'I can't do it without a licence.'

I muttered something very unkind, which I was glad he did not hear. Then I threw him a line.

'This is an emergency – the harbour master won't object.'

He grunted without conviction, but I was relieved to see that he was fastening his end of the line to his thwart. Five minutes later, we were safely hitched to a mooring a hundred and fifty yards away.

'Thank you very much', I said. 'We're very grateful. Can we give you something?'

'No, thanks. It's all right.'

'Have a packet of cigarettes, then.'

He shook his head firmly.

'No, thanks. I can't. That would be payment – and I haven't got a licence.'

With that, our rescuer departed in a surge of wake and conscience, leaving us to spend the next half hour tidying up the boat while we waited the arrival of officialdom from the shore, seventy yards away. One way and another, the morning was producing the most problematical and protracted exercise we had for some time – and all for the sake of posting a letter or two.

The bay was dominated by the large, white Government offices,

flying the Union Jack to remind the island's every visitor that St
Helena is still a British colony. Beyond the Government offices, we
could see the red, white, blue and green rooftops of Jamestown, the
island's only town. The south end of Jamestown ended abruptly
with some awesome cliffs which dropped perpendicularly into the
sea. To the north was Monden Hill, rising almost vertically to its
summit, nine hundred feet above. Carved out of the hillside was the
road to the top, winding its way upwards until it blended with the
barren ground and disappeared.

Along the concrete wharf at the north-eastern side of the bay
there was all the evidence of an extremely busy port. Baggage was
being loaded into lighters from hand-operated cranes. Dinghies
and motor vessels, moored in line astern, bobbed up and down in
the slight but constant swell.

Eventually, a rowing boat with a coloured man at the oars came
alongside us, carrying a very official and very solemn party of three,
each with his own sphere of authority and his own set of rules
and regulations for us to abide by. They stepped on board, but once
the introductions were over, any idea we might have had of getting
in a spot of sparkling conversation more or less dropped dead.

They brought with them a sort of weighty gloom which rapidly
caught Maureen and me in its net, struggle though we might to
introduce the social chit-chat. In the end, we had to fall in with the
spirit of the occasion, taking our cue from the glum chums and
generally exuding an impression of despair which would not have
come amiss in an insomniac who was urging his five thousandth
sheep over the water jump. Any undertaker in search of a bunch
of bearers who could be relied on not to whistle *Tipperary* while
carrying out their duties would have signed us on without a tremor.
The nearest we came to having a bright interlude was when one of
our visitors sighed like an east wind through a colander and pointed
out that we had parked at somebody else's mooring and would
we kindly move elsewhere immediately.

In the absence of any wind, the harbour launch towed us to
where we would not upset anybody, after which we gathered that
the encounter could now be considered as concluded. So we got a
lift ashore and lost no time in posting our letters once our passports
had been stamped and the Government offices had changed a cheque
for us. We had a look round the shops and invested in a range of
things from fresh food and a replacement table knife to a set of

snakes and ladders.

At the Government offices, we met Wilfred Millard, the Colonial Treasurer, and he invited us to his home for lunch, with the idea that he and his wife, Pam, would take us on a tour of the island in the afternoon. Maureen's hopes of finding a hairdresser before we went were quickly dashed when her first hopeful plea for directions to the salon was answered with the assurance that St Helena did not have a hairdresser.

On the other hand, finding a taxi to take us back with our provisions to the wharf was the simplest undertaking imaginable. There are more than four hundred cars on the island and most of their owners register them as taxis by paying an extra pound on their road tax. They hope to recoup it by obtaining a sliver of such unsubstantial business as is open to taxis on St Helena.

At the wharf, I re-filled twelve empty jerrycans with fresh water from a tank while Maureen loaded the stores into the rowing boat which had become temporarily ours in return for our mooring fee. While we were there, we discovered that the activity upon which we had already remarked was largely on account of the expected arrival that evening of the ship which called there once a month with mail and frozen food. The coloured man ferried us across to the yacht, where we unloaded the boat and had a quick wash before making the return trip to keep our appointment with our hosts for the afternoon – who, we found, had been on the island only six months of their scheduled two-year tour of duty.

We started our inspection of the 47 square miles with Wilfred Millard at the wheel of his car. It was remarkably easy to be impressed by the rugged terrain which lay below us once we had begun to make our way across the unproductive hills on roads where passing is possible only at certain places – with the driver who is going uphill having the right of way. The island is to all intents and purposes split into two by a mountain range from which project spurs, each divided by the deep chasms which take the streams down to the sea. There is hardly a gentle slope among them : they all seem to rise almost vertically to the top or to come to abrupt ends at the sea, as if some unseen hand has been unduly active with an outsize cake-knife.

All round us, we saw the barren volcanic rock, the harshness of the hillsides being broken only by the isolated copse or by wild fields of flax which had been left to their own devices since the island's industry collapsed with the introduction of man-made fibres. At the south-western end of St Helena, we met Lot and Lot's Wife – two fantastic towers of basalt, about two hundred and a hundred and sixty feet tall resectively. In Ruper's Bay, to the north, we saw signs of the third – and largely unsuccessful – attempt to start a fishing industry based on crayfish; and we met a man and two children collecting sand by wading out to sea and digging it from between the rocks, with the object of selling it to the Government for twenty-seven and six a cubic yard. Rupert's Bay is one of the two places on St Helena where sand can be found for the building industry.

It was a memorable day. By the end of it, we had seen Napoleon's tomb, the Governor's house, the French consul's house; learned the local employment statistics; found that islanders who consider going to the other side of St Helena from Jamestown refer to the undertaking as Going Foreign; seen that the social life is served by one cinema, two public houses and a fortnightly dance, with the European population helping things along with parties whenever parties are practicable; taken in the hard facts of survival for an economy which was propped by a British Government annual grant of a quarter of a million pounds.

We had dinner with Wilf and Pam, who gave us the key of their town flat and allowed us to spend the night there. Hot baths followed by a real bed should have ensured the sleep of a lifetime. Oddly, they did not. I supposed we missed the accustomed discomforts of a pitching bunk.

Next morning, Sunday, November 10, I went out for the bread we had ordered – having ascertained that it was baked only every second day – while Maureen prepared the breakfast. Afterwards, we watched the Remembrance Day parade pass our window. I had hoped to go diving and have a look at one of the wrecks which lie in the bay, because Supt Frank Martin, head of the island's police force – one inspector, one sergeant, ten constables – and I had found that diving was our common denominator as a result of his spotting my Smiths' Astral diving watch. This had to go by the board, however, because when we called at his home with Wilf and Pam we discovered that his air bottles were all empty. By the time we had finished charging them after lunch, it was 1700 hours – and we wanted to be out of the harbour before dusk. So we stayed and had dinner instead.

They all came with us to the wharf, where we realized that there was a very little wind. Frank suggested that a tow would not come amiss, so he and the others got into Frank's motorized dinghy while I dropped our moorings and threw them the line. At 1800 hours, we were on our way, leaving behind us in the gathering dusk a wharf on which the only excitement was now a children's football match. Within a couple of minutes, we had picked up the wind, so I yelled to Frank that we could now take care of ourselves.

Hurried goodbyes followed my raising of the sail, then *Dytiscus* began to gather speed as she harvested the breeze. Soon, she was skipping along at five knots on a north-westerly course out of the bay, and we were slipping easily into the sailing routine again after our thirty-six-hour break. St Helena was already an island of memories, many of which we would not easily forget.

One such memory was Billy Stevens, an islander who broadcast three times a week on his own commercial radio station. For an unextortionate threepence a time, he would play anybody's record request. Provided, naturally, that he happened to have the record.

The lights of Jamestown were still visible when, after ninety minutes' sailing, we had the first incident of our resumed voyage. A self-steering gear line snapped, leaving me the alternatives of lowering sail or asking Number One to take the tiller so that we could continue to make progress while I repaired it. I chose Number One.

We were still doing five knots, and we were goose-winged, but she kept us ploughing on without a suspicion of a gybe until the self-steering gear was ready to take over again.

12

Alarm at the line

Chay Blyth : November 11 – November 25

*T*HE drawback to having a cook on board is that you tend to
make the most of mealtimes. Meals the Maureen way were
meals which defied me to miss a morsel. They sat on my plate,
packed to the gills with vitamins and jollying along an appetite
which it was a pleasure to own. The snag was that their sheer
presentability, allied to the fact of my being a compulsive eater
anyway, was beginning to have its effect on my shape. Three months
at sea on my own had produced Blyth, the raw-boned mariner with
the lean and hungry look; the month which had passed since
Maureen joined had filled in the hollows, rounded off the
corners and given me the sleek appearance of a citizen for whom
times were good. I would not go so far as to say that I had moved
from the raw-boned to the roly-poly, but certainly I could not
pretend that I was not aware of the approach of pudginess.

Chips had begun to take an honoured place on the menu – and
chips mean as much to me as Highland Toffee! I resolved in my
log of November 13 : 'The only time I will ever be sailing solo
again is in the Single-handed Transatlantic Race or if I go round
the world non-stop. If I have to go to the Isle of Wight, I shall
make sure there is someone with me. It is not because of the loneliness, because I enjoy that – but the other person makes you eat
that little bit better and the place tends to be more "livable".'

By this time, we were seven days behind the schedule which
was necessary for us to be home for Christmas. But at least the
winds which had at last sprung up were showing no signs of leaving
us, which was just as well : I reckoned we now had to do at least
a hundred miles a day if we were to make Plymouth – Britain's
nearest port and the goal we had set ourselves – in time to get in a
train journey to Newcastle before December 25.

All the time, Number One was finding out more about sailing.

154

Several times, when the self-steering gear broke, she took the tiller with complete confidence; she commented approvingly on the strength of the boat's fittings; she got to grips with the sextant when it was time for a noon sight, and showed every sign of her eventual mastery of it in spite of complaining that she kept losing the sun. And although she protested that every boat should have a sewing machine, she made a far better job of patching the ghosting genoa than I could have done. Admittedly, explaining time by longitude seemed to sow confusion within her – but there was plenty of opportunity yet for her to sort it out. Every time I settled down to plot our position, she was at my shoulder, anxious to see the results of our calculations.

She was there one morning when she happened to look out of the window above the chart table – and suddenly produced a startled cry.

'A ship! A ship!'

She had every cause for excitement. The merchant tanker which was a mere eight hundred feet away was the first ship we had seen since we had passed Table Mountain, twenty-seven days earlier. It looked enormous because it was so long since we had been so close to one. I switched on the radio in case it tried to contact us – but it did not. It headed off towards South Africa across a sea which had become a deep, inviting blue, compared with the greyish green of the last few days. The day held every promise of being a scorcher.

Sure enough, within three hours and before mid-day, the temperature was eighty-eight degrees in the saloon and a hundred and sixteen in the cockpit. While Maureen skulked in the shade of the sails, I stripped off and treated myself to a sunbath. And despite Maureen's efforts to avoid the sun, her shoulders became very sore as the day wore on. I rubbed some cream in for her.

'Bit better?' I asked.

She did not reply for a moment. She just sat, looking out across the heaving sea, which was begining to seem increasingly purposeful and was keeping us busy by tossing flying fish on to the deck.

'Don't worry', she said.

I was intrigued.

'What do you mean?'

'About me. You don't have to worry about me. I'm all right.'

'I'm not worrying . . . .'

'I think you are. These last few days, you haven't been able to do enough for me. Nothing seems too much trouble. I think you're trying to convince yourself that you didn't ask too much when you cabled me to come out to South Africa and sail back with you. I think you were a bit taken aback when the people on St Helena were so surprised at my taking it on.'

I did not say anything; just rubbed her shoulders a bit more dedicatedly. The fact was, I was just a bit conscience-stricken when I considered the sheer impossibility of what I had asked – that my wife should leave our baby behind and come and rough it on a thirty-foot yacht until Christmas. All the same, it had been the chance of a lifetime . . . .

'You didn't ask too much, Chay. A woman's place is by her husband's side. All the same, it would have been nice if Samantha had been a little bit older – then she could have come as well!'

'That really would have been something,' I said. 'But she would have had to be quite a bit older. Even the Blyths can't start taking on an under-school age crew.'

I paused; grinned my gratitude at her.

'Maureen, you're marvellous.'

And so, of course, she was. There were times when she was frightened, when rogue waves thundered upon us as the seas went on growing – and I knew she thought the boat seemed to be sinking a lot lower in the water than it used to be. But she was sticking it without complaint, determined to overcome her fear and to master the skills which the sea demands of those who pit themselves against it, because the sea was working its timeless magic on her – a magic we could share in so many ways.

We leaned over the bow together to see the flashing phosphorescence of an evening school of dolphins, crossing and re-crossing in front of us like an underwater firework display; we offered scraps of food to the birds which wheeled about us with a tirelessly curving curiosity; we marvelled at the majesty of the increasing numbers of ships which were now coming our way. Two American frigates on a south-easterly course showed up, menacingly grey against the grey and choppy sea. Maureen hoisted the ensign – and the rear frigate responded by flying a Union Jack with its own Stars and Stripes.

We found Ascension Island on Saturday, November 16, which meant that we had covered seven hundred and three miles in the six days since we had left St Helena. A day later, it had disappeared behind us, but the weather was beginning to threaten a change : calms and squalls were replacing the reassuring winds which had been looking after us so well, and constant sail-changing became the order of the day. But I found time to remark that Maureen was keeping to her routine of making up her face each morning and putting rollers in her hair at night. She seemed surprised that I should have mentioned it.

'I must look pretty for you', she said. 'I do at home, so why not here?'

It was a good question, and for the life of me I could not think of an answer to it as I made the night drinks which emptied our first tin of drinking chocolate. Unfortunately, the sunshine had not been helping her. The soreness on her shoulders had developed into a rash of broken blisters on her back and chest and was spreading down her arms, despite two-hourly bathes with diluted antiseptic.

We decided on a course of tetracycline and vitamin B tablets, in the hope of sorting things out. I did think about trying some home-grown penicillin on her when we found that our last seven loaves of bread had gone mouldy. 'I'll eat the inside and leave you the crusts,' I said – but she did not seem keen, so I threw the lot overboard to give the fishes a treat.

By Tuesday, Maureen was distinctly groggy. She got up at 0730 hours but was back in bed again ninety minutes later, complaining that her legs had developed jelly-like tendencies. She spent most of the day in the saloon, although it was stiflingly hot there : it was still eighty-eight degrees at 1800 hours. The noon sight put us at 4° 40′ South, 17° 40′ West, so I promised to throw Number One in when we reached the Equator – which possibly was not a suggestion to be mistaken for the show of husbandly sympathy that the situation quite obviously demanded.

Next day, however, she was fighting fit again : spotty, admittedly, but sprightly. It was just as well, because it was a day it would have been a shame for her to miss. We awoke to blazing sunshine and we had our breakfast in the cockpit while we listened to the world news on the B.B.C. Overseas Service. A Portuese man o' war went floating by, pink and placid in the sparkling surface. By 1100 hours, the temperature in the saloon was ninety-one degrees and the cockpit was virtually red hot, so we established ourselves on the coach roof, which was just high enough to catch the breeze.

The noon sight showed that we had travelled a hundred and forty-two miles in twenty-four hours, which was further than any day had pushed me since my departure from the Hamble. I was taking the sight when a tremendous crowd of dolphins arrived. There must have been about a hundred of them, and they were bigger than any I had previously seen – some of them fifteen feet long, which made me wonder if they could perhaps be baby whales.

Many of them had huge scars on their backs, as if they had been fighting, and there was one pitted with ulcers the size of a cup. Maureen was not too happy when I finished my roll of film and had to go below for a new one. She had visions of being alone on deck and finding that the boat was being attacked.

'I *know* they're supposed to be playful,' she howled at me. 'But *do they* know?'

She was even more impressed when I called to her to join me in the saloon, to listen to a strange, high-pitched grinding noise, all mixed up with a sucking and a squeaking, coming from the bottom of the boat. Our visitors were hitting the side and scratching themselves on the hull: they would presumably have even more scars to show the next boat that passed. We stood quite still for several minutes, enthralled by the eerie excitement. Then we went back on deck, where I tried some more photographs. Maureen, I could see, could hardly believe the splashing pantomime which was going on all round us. She was enchanted; excited as a toddler at a toy fair.

'Chay, they're marvellous! Oo, look at that one over there. Isn't he *huge!*'

These were splendid days: the sun blazing down, the wind filling the sails, *Dytiscus* skimming along like a boat which was at last enjoying being a boat, after the undeserved tribulations which had come her way since June 8. The trouble was the temperatures – in the nineties regularly in the saloon, and up to a hundred and fourteen degrees in the cockpit. The fibreglass deck felt red hot, and whenever we wanted to sit down it was necessary to sluice buckets of sea water over it first to cool it off a bit. The other trouble was lack of exercise: the winds came steadily from the south-east, and we had the sails boomed out and more or less left *Dytiscus* to it. We had the sun behind us, which meant that shade was virtually non-existent, so we drank our way steadily through pepsi and lemonade and talked our way through our plans for the future. Maureen was not exactly brimming with enthusiasm over the Andes as another possible manifestation of Blyth unpredict-ability, so I kept off that one most of the time. We confined our calculations instead to the 1972 solo transatlantic race and one or two other possibilities. I kept pegging away at the idea of Maureen's entering. I am afraid that once I get my teeth into a notion I do not give either it or the person I am hoping to convince much of a rest. If I think a cause is good, I tend to preach it loud and long – and I was certain that Maureen would prove completely capable of taking on the Atlantic single-handed. She was now able to plot our course, and we went over the radio again and on to the uses and purposes of flares and how to tell which way a ship is going at night when you cannot make out its port and starboard lights – which was something I had picked up in *English Rose*.

I was delighted with her progress; fascinated at hearing the way she had begun to trot out nautical terms in general conversation, when such things had been a foreign language to both of us until a few months ago – and to Maureen until only a week or so back; appalled at the thought that she would probably end up by beating me once battle had been joined.

At present, however, the only battle was with the sun, which was by now setting about us with a dedication which made its previous efforts fade into comparative insignificance. On November 22, when we were just ninety miles south of the Equator, the cabin temperature reached ninety-seven degrees and the cockpit was a sizzling hundred and twenty-eight. We both felt completely ener-vated. Any carefully nurtured kitten could have pushed us over. We had begun taking vitamin pills, to try to pep ourselves up a bit, as *Dytiscus* sped on without our assistance.

The following day brought its own tonic. We crossed the line at 1335 hours, beneath a sun which was blazing out of an incredible blue sky, untouched by the slightest suspicion of cloud. It was the sort of day that office workers everywhere dream about. Maureen's dreams, I am afraid, had been more like nightmares ever since I had promised her that I would throw her in on Equator Day. She is not the best of swimmers, and she was quite plainly a bit aghast at the thought of finding herself alongside *Dytiscus* with her legs about three miles too short for her to stand on. I resolved to jolly her along a bit: nobody is likely to confuse me with the celebrated Sir Galahad.

Number One', I said, all rasp and promise. 'Come here!'

She eyed me with distinct concern from her spot on the saloon roof, but made no effort to jump to attention.

'What?' she asked. Unnecessarily: she knew what.

'It's time we had a little ceremony . . . .'

'Chay!'

'You know I always keep a promise, don't you?'

'Chay!'

I advanced towards her, leering like a left-over from a Boris Karlof bonanza.

'Just a little ceremony, Maureen . . . .'

Before she could blink, I grabbed her round the waist and pulled her to the side, down off the roof.

'Only a little ceremony . . . .'

'You big oaf! Stop it!'

'A little ceremony', I puffed: she was making a fight of it. 'Like this . . . .'

And I loosed her in order to stretch my legs over the side and dangle my feet in the water. She looked like a Roman Christian who had got into the Coleseum and been told that the lions had just dined.

'Chay, you beast!'

Then she slipped down beside me and by stretching determinedly she managed to splash her feet in the sea as well. It was a crazy, delirious moment. We splashed the sea and we splashed each other, and we laughed like a couple of chars on a Blackpool outing. We both knew it was a moment we were going to remember for a long time to come.

Then we had lunch on the saloon roof, where the mainsail was offering grateful shade. Ham, onions, chutney, mustard, cream crackers – and the bottle of South African wine that I had been itching to get at since we had brought it aboard. We drank a toast to Father Neptune, and one to ourselves, and one to Samantha, and one to our friends, and one to the solo transatlantic. The snag was, the measure had to shrink considerably to enable the wine to keep pace with inspiration. Much as I admired the thought behind the gesture, I could not help thinking Maureen was taking the festive season a bit far when she threw a mouthful over the side for Davy Jones. We sat and talked until 1600 hours, by which time we were feeling wonderfully idle and drowsy. So we treated ourselves to

an hour's siesta while the tape recorder offered the empty ocean
The Sound of Music, pianissimo.

At dinner that night, we rounded off our celebrations by a toast
in whisky. According to my calculations, we had arrived at the
Equator a week later than was healthy for our home-for-Christmas
target – but having arrived at all was a circumstance which defied
us to resist rejoicing. For me, there was also a much more tangible
reason for feeling that life this magic evening was all that I could
possibly hope for : the wonderful girl who had made it possible
in the first place, both by agreeing to my setting off solo and then
by flying out to join me when I was thinking that fate had kicked
me in the teeth. I looked at her across the top of my glass of Dewar's,
pretty as a picture, grey-blue eyes sparkling in the pert face, and
I thanked God again for the partner He had given me. It was a
night of stars in a black velvet heaven; a night to be grateful for,
for the rest of our lives; a night for murmured confidences as the
black sea hissed by.

I took hold of the small brown hand and leaned towards its
owner.

'Maureen, there's something I want you to know . . . .'

I paused, and in the silence we heard the sea speaking to
Dytiscus. Then :

'It's a pity it wasn't a bit calmer earlier on – then I *would* have
thrown you in.'

* * * * * *

The next day, reaction set in– helped by the fact that at 0915
hours we crossed the route I had taken on my journey southwards
about eighteen weeks earlier, when I had gone crashing in pursuit
of John Ridgway. A couple of weeks before that, when I had been
near the Cape Verde Islands, I had apparently been two hundred
miles behind him, so we must have been very close by the time
I reached the point to which I had now returned.

It was a nostalgic day, full of memomries of a pell-mell pursuit.
It had been a chase which had put *Dytiscus* through her paces in a
way which I was sure would have made Ronald Nierop blench if
he had been able to see its demands on his tough but unpretentious
family cruiser. Because of the boat's extraordinary strength, I had
felt confident in keeping more canvas up than I should have done if
I had thought she could not take it – and somehow she had risen

F

to the challenge. The odd thing was that on this return journey, with the nonsensical pressure off, a bottle screw had parted, a stanchion had smashed, and she had collected a hole in the deck. Somebody, I was more sure than ever, had been looking after me on that rodeo ride south, as I careered on in blind faith and ignorance.

Somebody, that is to say, and *Dytiscus* herself – as strong a boat as I could have wished for, even if she did have to bow to the extortionate demands of the Roaring Forties in the end. The pace of my approach run had not exactly helped, either, by getting me into the forties in the winter instead of the spring. And it was ironical that I had started earlier than I had originally intended, so as not to give John too much of a start. Perhaps if I had stuck to my plan, started later and taken it easier, I would have stayed out of trouble. Perhaps, perhaps. But on the other hand, if I had still been swishing solo past Australia I would have been missing the chance of sharing a voyage with Maureen – the opportunity of a lifetime, marred only by the unavoidable absence of little Number Two. I had much to be grateful for, I thought, as I watched Maureen getting on with some washing in the cockpit while the temperature sat steadily at something over a hundred.

It was when the washing was finished and she was getting the fruits of her labours sorted out for drying that she suddenly shouted 'Oh, blast it!' loudly and with feeling. She had dropped a towel overboard.

'Never mind', I said. 'Davy Jones will probably be glad of it if he spilled some of that wine you gave him yesterday.'

Whatever he had done with the wine, Davy Jones was certainly spilling some water. We had sprung enough leaks to make us the envy of the most competently constructed colander, and the saloon floor was constantly wet. I got on my hands and knees to mop up in a temperature of ninety-two degrees. I also fiddled inefficiently with the cooker, which had developed the unsociable habit of turning all the utensils black and vomitting smoke at the sligheest provocation. I snarled unkindly at it.

Fortunately, it was Sunday – wash and shave day. So I washed and I shaved, and I was delighted that this simple process could still achieve a morale-boosting miracle. By the time I had finished, I felt at peace with the world again.

Peace did not last very long. The Doldrums gave us their first squall at 0200 hours next day, as if to make sure that we realized we were now in this most uncertain of areas, where nature throws tempers for fifteen minutes and sulks without breathing for days. We fell out of bed in a pantomime for two, and I struggled into my oilskins while the saloon bucked and rolled like a switchback on overtime. On deck, I found the wind throwing fits in the rigging while the sea lumbered monstrously aboard every other minute and the rain lashed me with a fusillade of needles. Swearing and sliding about the glassy deck, I managed eventually to raise the storm jib and lower the mainsail. Then, as quickly as the tantrum had started, it died down, and we spent the rest of the night balancing between wakefulness and sleep, uneasy for the next onslaught. The next onslaught never came : round one of the cat and mouse game to the Doldrums.

By breakfast time, we were back to our heatwave – and immediately after that we were back to cooker-blasting. It refused unrepentantly to burn cleanly. Greasy, sooty smoke belch forth with black abandon. I could see no alternative to stripping it completely down, while Maureen set about trying to scrub its filthy aftermath off the pans and the galley walls and ceiling.

It was a joyless exercise in a temperature of ninety-two degrees. Screws had rusted solid and I ripped the heads off two of them in my sweat-splashed struggles. Tempers rose in time with the temperature, because Number One was having as little success as I was. Pans clanked, hammers flew. Bangs and clatters failed to conceal the cordiality of my curses. I raised hell with the cooker, Maureen lambasted the galley, and we each found time to criticize the other. Finally, however, our struggles were rewarded when we tried the cooker again and it condescended to shoot forth a blue flame. Just as well, really : I am sure that if it had not done so, *I* would have. And Maureen gave praise for my genius and I extolled her patience with the galley, and we decided we were both glad to have the other about after all.

It had been our first fight of the voyage, and making up made it all worth while. Soon afterwards, we were drinking coffee as if nothing had happened.

13

One more for the Sea Lark

Maureen Blyth : November 26 – December 12

NOVEMBER 26 was my fiftieth day at sea, but it did not seem grateful for this distinction. On the contrary, it behaved appallingly, like a day which knew just how bad-mannered a Doldrums day should be. The morning frowned about us with heavy clouds and not a breath of wind : a sullen morning which could not even raise a smile at the futility of our hopes to make some progress. We bobbed gently up and down on a sleeping sea, and the only excitement came when I nearly managed to amputate two fingers. I was trying to get the key into the lunchtime sardine tin when my fingers slipped and the flap of the tin slashed straight across my knuckles.

Soon after mid-day, Day 50 lost its temper. The first squall hit us – and signalled the first of the dozens of sail changes which were to follow. Chay and I were up on deck continuously until 6 p.m., when I went below to make supper. By that time, it had been raining for four hours – raining with an intensity I had never seen before. It simply lashed down, and every now and again, without warning, the boat would shoot along like a streak of lightning.

The self-steering gear just could not control it, and she would go over on her side like a wounded animal. Then Chay would be fighting the tiller in the blinding downpour to try to ease her back. The waves were quite small, because the seas had not had time to build up, but they were streaked with foam. And whatever direction we looked in, there was a haze of splashing rain, six inches high, across the surface of the water. Not that we could see very far : the visibility was hardly worth talking about. And when an electric storm came along as well, I was absolutely terrified. I found it very hard to concentrate on helping Chay with the sails as we went through a series of permutations, right down to storm jib only. The rain kept coming, although the wind died and disappeared

164

time after time. That meant that instead of being buffetted and wet we were just plain wet – with nothing to distract us from a full appreciation of how wet we were. By the end of the day, we were both whacked. When Chay slumped on to his bunk and said 'Damn the Doldrums', he meant every syllable.

The next day was much the same, except that the leaden sky did not produce its first downpour until 5 p.m., and the wind did not swell the sails until three hours after that. It was hot and it was humid, and we sat on the saloon roof watching a school of beautiful fish, three feet long, leaping out of the water all round us. They were dark on their backs, with pale blue sides and gold underbellies, and Chay pointed the camera hopefully in their direction with the idea of having evidence to support some of the memories we would take back home.

And what memories they would be. The voyage was a sort of second honeymoon —except that the first one, which we spent at Gullane, on the Firth of Forth, could not compare with it.

The splendour of the sea, the wondrously assorted creatures that live in it – ranging from the tiny flying fish to the twenty-foot long whale which the Doldrums now produced for us – and the breathtaking wonder of moonlight on the ocean were things I had never dreamed of when I stepped aboard *Dytiscus* at Port Elizabeth.

I was missing little Samantha terribly, of course, but even the dreadful void which had become part of my life the day I kissed her goodbye in Newcastle could not prevent my realizing that the sea had a magnetism all of its own. The Doldrums, as Chay said, were enough to drive anybody dotty with their unpredictability – but the sea was by no means all Doldrums and I was able now to see what it is that calls men to it, away from the rat race of life on land. I was able, too, to appreciate more fully the sort of hell it must have given Chay and John when they dared the Atlantic in *English Rose*. A true understanding was impossible – there must be a world of difference between facing a force ten storm in a thirtyfoot yacht, when you are three or four feet away from the water, and facing two hurricanes in a twenty-foot rowing boat when the water is a mere nine inches below you – but at least I was on the way to getting the message; at least I had seen something.

Try as I might, I could not imagine a hurricane. I was sure there could be nothing worse than a storm. The realization that there was in fact even more to the powers of nature than what

I had seen filled me with a sense of horrified fascination. I had been impressed when Chay had come home from the Atlantic and had told me the sort of things that he had gone through, but I had really had no idea of the implication of his words. Now that I had been given an insight, and even allowing for the fact that I was bound to be biased because Chay was my husband, I was filled with admiration.

I do not think I would say it went as far as hero-worship – probably because I do not like the expression, which seems to me to suggest that I am hanging on because he has done so much – but you could not squeeze more admiration out of me if you tried.

Squeezing patience, on the other hand, was virtually impossible for a different reason : for four days, after the final squall had subsided, we were becalmed. Patience became a rare commodity : as far as we were concerned, there was hardly any patience left to be squeezed. One day, morbid curiosity prompted Chay to take a sight – but as this revealed that we had covered the princely distance of eighteen miles in twenty-four hours he decided not to enquire further as long as *Dytiscus* simply continued to bob. It would be difficult for anyone who has never experienced the sensation of drifting helplessly on an empty sea, a thousand miles from land, to imagine the build-up of the awareness of an over-whelming futility as day follows day, each one more frustrating than the last. The nothingness of it all becomes oppressive – even on a second honeymoon which offers a bonus of a complete double rain-bow above a mirror sea, as this one did on the fourth day of the calms. We got down to the realization that being back with Samantha for Christmas might mean cutting short our sail at the Azores and flying home, leaving the yacht to be shipped in our wake.

'Damn the Doldrums!' That was Chay again. He had rather cottoned on to what was an extremely appropriate catchphrase. 'At least when you're in a rowing boat you can row!'

And yet, as so often happened, when we were really feeling sorry for ourselves, Nature organized a two-stage rescue act. We had more or less resigned ourselves to the idea of being permanent prisoners of a bobbing boat in the blistering equatorial heat, when the rain returned. A tremendous evening downpour gave the sea's surface a sandstorm haze as the waters of the heavens and the earth met in a million collisions all round us. With the rain came a wonderful, reviving freshness. It was as if somebody above had looked over my shoulder the previous night, when I wrote in my hard-backed exercise book log: 'Another blistering day. It's dreadful to be running in sweat all the time, from morning until night. Your clothes are absolutely wringing and it's so humid. I am so looking forward, when I get home, to having a long bath with lots and lots of bath oil; then to covering myself with my favourite French perfume, *Replique,* and to dressing once again like a woman and to feeling and smelling nice again.'

Perhaps I still could not have a bath with lots of bath oil, and a small yacht was no place for dressing like a woman – shorts and check shirts were much more practical propositions – but at least I could revel in the cleanness of the rain.

'Chay – I'm going to have a rainbath!'

Clothes off. Grab a bar of soap. Into the cockpit. Lift my face to the skies and welcome the rain with open arms. Then give myself to the sheer luxury of an all-over soaping, feeling despair falling from me along with the heat and the perspiration which are beating a rapid retreat in the face of the thoroughness of Nature's own showerbath. And now Chay is beside me, whooping like an extra in a cowboys-and-indians picture as he captures the sheer delirium of having heaven wash him. I join the chorus: *'Alloo-alloo-alloo!'*

We were like a latterday nymph and shepherd. Or perhaps Chay was a chubby cherub, large economy size and dripping with raindrops. What mattered was that we were a nymph and shepherd renewed, a cherub with his chippiness back. We felt we could look the Doldrums in the eye again. We scampered below to towel ourselves tingling-dry and we proclaimed our readiness to face tomorrow, whatever depths tomorrow sank to. And this, though we could not know it at that moment, was merely Stage One of Nature's rescue act.

Stage Two started at ten o'clock next morning with a whisper of a breeze from the north-east. Chay did a spot more whooping.

'I think we may have found the trades', he shouted, holding up a moistened stubby forefinger for confirmation of his hopes. We hoisted the ghoster and the mainsail, and the breeze developed in its own good time to force two. For the rest of the day, we were skimming north-west at about four knots, intermittently chirruping at each other with the exhilaration of being on the move again. The sunshine was warm but not overpowering, and we relaxed on the saloon roof – moving into the cockpit only for lunch and dinner. Dinner was a meal in the moonlight: wonderful! As the days had passed, Chay's South American hopes had begun to find their way into our conversation more and more. And now we talked again about the Andes and the Amazon, and all the things that would be necessary if the idea were to reach maturity. Chay was going through all the familiar motions of getting the thing on paper – plans, problems, possibilities – but somehow I still had the feeling that he was not altogether committed to it. Time, I decided, would tell.

By the time we went to bed, shortly before midnight, the wind had risen to force four. And again we had the feeling that things were looking up.

We were awakened at 3.30 a.m. because the boat was keeling well over on its side. We discovered we were crashing through an inky night which was being repeatedly lit by lightning flashes and grumbled at by horrendous thunderclaps. I was terrified, but I went on deck with Chay to help him to lower the ghoster while the wind drove rain into our faces like hundreds of very sharp needles, and the black sea crashed against and over the boat. My main function was to hold the torch so that Chay could see what he was doing, but I am afraid it was the shakiest of searchlights. The ghoster was no sooner down than the wind rose to even greater efforts. Chay yelled above it: 'I'll have to drop the main as well.' So I went on holding the torch and trying to stop dithering with fright. I had the absurd urge to close my eyes every time a sheet of lightning dropped into the sky like a fried egg spreading across a blackened pan, with Chay and the howling rigging and the furious waves silhouetted fleetingly against it. I do not like lightning at the best of times, and when I am its only possible target in a thousand square miles of sea I like it even less. For the rest of the night, while we lay a-hull, I did my ostrich act in my bunk, tucking my head down inside my sleeping bag so that I could not see the fireworks outside. *Maureen Blyth, you'll never be a sailor!*

The curious thing was, I still wanted to find out for myself if I *could* be, despite the fears that were built in to the very idea. The thought of being on deck alone on a night like this one absolutely gave me the shudders. Portsmouth was a much more comfortable place than the Atlantic Ocean. And to think that Chay had been through something far worse than this in a little rowing boat! boat!

Nevertheless, something inside me was telling me I had got to try; reminding me that the sea was not always like this; that the sea was often smooth and kind and magical, and that at such times, given a fair wind, sailing was something magical, too. Chay wanted me to try the solo transatlantic race in 1972 : it was his favourite theme and he had been returning repeatedly for the last month, prodding away at it with words of encouragement about the progress he said I was making, or just letting slip the odd remark as if he had reached the stage of taking my entry for granted. When Chay gives his all to a gospel, the person on the receiving end just has to acknowledge the apparent inevitability of it all. And what with Chay's chatter and my own first-hand evidence of the pleasures which sailing could offer on the good days, I was aware that I had already reached the point where I was not prepared to dismiss the solo transatlantic race out of hand. Perhaps at this stage it was only a possibility – but when I stepped aboard *Dytiscus* on October 8 it had not even been that!

Perversely, it was conditions like the ones which were making me an ostrich which were adding a bit of backbone to that possibility. While the thunder rolled and the lightning flashed and *Dytiscus* took her battering, I reminded myself that Chay had come through much worse than this – and something unaccountable inside me wanted me to show him that a woman could do as well as he could. *Maureen, you're as mad as your husband!*

I thought I had already learned enough to enable me to manage a thirty-foot yacht or perhaps a slightly large one, but I still needed to back with experience the rudiments of the groundwork I had gained in my nine weeks as crew to Captain Blyth. In any case, the basic requirement for the solo transatlantic race was that entrants should have completed five hundred miles of single-handed sailing. I had also to overcome my qualms about the dark, which never troubled me at home but which I found utterly eerie at sea if ever I was on deck by myself. And I had an illogical – feminine, Chay would say! – horror of the phosphorescence of fish at night.

But above all, there was Samantha. I was the mother of the most wonderful little girl in the world. Having discovered the ache of being without her on the present trip, could I steel myself to a six-week separation in 1972, when she would be five years old and able to worry about where Mummy was and whether Mummy was all right? Things would not be as simple for Samantha in 1972

as they had been when Chay was away for the first four months
of the present trip. We had a big photograph of Chay in the
bedroom, and every night before she went to bed it was 'Goodnight,
Daddy' and 'Give Daddy a kiss.' Or it was 'Where's Daddy?' and
she would look straight at that photograph, with all the alertness
that a non-talking toddler could master.

I used to try to teach her a little saying, thinking that she would
be talking very well when Chay came home. *Please look after
Daddy, that he will stay home with Mummy*. We did not get very
far with that – and now Mummy had gone away as well and was
thinking about going away some more! What a crazy, confused
business it all was!

The thunder reverberated again. I went on being an ostrich.

The following day was December 1. The change of month
seemed to make Christmas all the nearer, and when the wind
dropped at about ten o'clock in the morning, leaving us becalmed
again, we decided it was time to make a firm change of plan. The
Azores, which until now had been a sort of insurance in our minds
while our sights were set on Plymouth, had now to become our
target. They were a long way away, but they were obviously the
only hope we had of being home for Christmas. We had no money
with us, but Chay said he was sure the British Consul would be
able to arrange our air passage to England on a fly-now-pay-later
system.

Chay sorted out his North Atlantic charts and decided he had
one which would see us safely to the Azores. At about tea-time,
the wind made its first move to take us there. With its return, my
hopes for Christmas rose again. Perhaps even now we would be
able to see S.F.'s eyes light up when she saw the tricycle we had
bought her as her Christmas present when whe were in the middle
of the panic to get Chay on his way. The next day, we were fairly
rocketing along, keeled over at thirty degrees to port nearly the
whole time. It was a day for raising our spirits – but it was not
altogether a good day for Chay. He christened it Losing Day. It
started with my discovery that the ghosting genoa, in its sail bag,
had fallen into the water and was trailing behind us – still with us
only by virtue of the fact that Chay had tied it to the guard rails
the night before.

I shouted for Chay, who was in the middle of taking a sight.
He put the sextant into its box in the cockpit and pushed his Astral

diving watch – which played an important part in his navigational calculations – into his anorak pocket. Then he leaned over the side to pull the sail aboard – and lost the watch out of his pocket. Fortunately, if there was one thing which we were not short of, it was watches. Then, a bit later on, while washing out the polythene bucket which was our nearest approach to mod. cons. because of the decision to do without a toilet for the sake of having more storage space, Chay managed to drop that overboard as well.

'Chay – it will be you next time! Do be careful!'

'Don't panic, Number One – we've got another one. And in any case, Davy Jones could probably do with a bucket, so that he can wring out the towel you gave him to mop up the wine you gave him!'

'Chay Blyth', I said firmly, 'you're a beast.'

'I know – and aren't you glad!'

This man of mine is utterly incorrigible. I told him so: 'You're incorrigible!' I should never have bothered. He turned to me like an innocent child.

'I thought you said that *encouraging* was what I never needed . . . .'

If there had been anything handy, I would have thrown it – even at the risk of giving it to Davy Jones.

We had about sixteen hundred miles to cover in seventeen days if we were to be at the Azores by December 20: that was the date we had decided we should aim at, in order to allow time for the formalities of landing and customs clearance and of explaining ourselves to the British Consul, and time after that for catching a plane home. And now, the weather seemed intent on helping.

Day after day, force five or six winds filled the sails and urged us on our way. *Dytiscus* responded splendidly, standing up to the big seas which built up in answer to the surge of the winds. Time after time, rogue waves swept over the deck; always, *Dytiscus* came up doing whatever is a thirty-foot yacht's equivalent of smiling. They were hot, sticky days. Chay declined a wash on the grounds that the slightest exertion made him sweat like a bull, so there did not really seem much point in having one. Even writing my log was hard work when the coolest place at 6.30 p.m. was the saloon – eighty-six degrees. We decided that the best policy was to stay on deck in our sailing suits, getting soaked by the sea, rather than stay below and achieve the same result on a do-it-yourself basis with perspiration.

We were, however, doing about a hundred miles a day, and we were noticeably moving into a cooler climate. Our progress would have been greater if the boat had not been carrying the fantastic amount of growth below the waterline – and this, despite the special anti-fouling solution with which she had been treated. I could not imagine what she would have been like without the treatment, but with it, she had barnacles on her barnacles. One day, Chay found that speedometer was not working. He pulled out the impellor to find what was wrong – and, sure enough, what he found was a barnacle. It must have been in there for weeks, tucked away in the hole in the hull, until it had finally grown big enough to stop the rotor turning. It did not take him long to throw out the intruder and restore normal service.

As long as the mountainous seas continued, we had visits from flying fish. Two of them, each about seven inches long, jumped into the cockpit. We threw them back before their frantic struggles had died.

We went on ploughing north, gradually being pushed to the west by the winds which continued to whip at us from the north-east. There was no let-up, either for *Dytiscus* or ourselves. At times, great blocks of green water thumped us like so many tons of concrete, and the port side went right under the waves as the boat keeled over. But at least the self-steering gear did not have to cope with the problems of running in front of the wind, so there was no difficulty from that quarter. Much as I was enjoying my first sea voyage, how I wished that Chay had not been thwarted in his hopes by the boat's inability to run well in heavy seas.

As I had waited in Newcastle, I had had the feeling that if he could get past South Africa he would get right round the world. I had been full of confidence for him until I received the letters which he had written aboard *Gillian Gaggins* at Tristan da Cunha and which had been sent on by Captain MacAlister. Then it became apparent that I had been too much of an optimist : too much had gone wrong between Madeira and Tristan. They were probably little things in themselves, but all put together they were a lot. It was after that that I began to think he was not going to get much further; after that I began to dread the arrival of the telegram boy. I did not want Chay to do anything foolish, and I knew I could trust him not to, but at the same time I prayed that he would achieve his goal for both our sakes : for his sake, because he was so set on it and because he had put so much into it, and for my sake, selfishly, because I thought that if he got round the world he might feel inclined to bring Blyth Adventures to an end and settle down to life at home with Samantha and me.

Most of his telegrams had dealt with specific points that had cropped up, like the eyebolts on his mast, the petrol contamination, and the rudder – so when I received one which showed that he had remembered Samantha's birthday I am afraid I suspected an ulterior motive. I said to myself : 'He's waiting to open the birthday parcel!' The point is, you see, Chay *never* remembers birthdays. I am sure he does not even know when his own is. Every year, about the first week in September, he writes to Mummy in Newcastle to ask when my birthday is, so that he can send me a card. I have got wise to it now. The week before, I always put a note on the dressing table mirror : 'Maureen's birthday, September 26.'

With his 'routine' telegrams – the ones that wanted me to check up on something or other – my course of action was simple and straightforward. Because I was up in Newcastle and all Chay's expert friends were on the south coast, I could not do much running around – so I used to telephone the people most likely to have the answer. Frank and Audrey Allen were a great help, and I am afraid Frank bore the brunt of my enquiries because I had his home telephone number – and the telegrams used to arrive in the evenings, when there would be nobody at any of the business numbers which I had noted in my diary. In any case, Frank was always the right person to ask : he was a mine of information. And when Chay sent me those little figures to give me his position, I had no idea what they meant, so I used to telephone Frank and he would say he is three hundred miles west of blah-blah-blah and translate it into English for me.

Chay and I had planned that I would spend a lot of time getting Ropelawshiel, the cottage in Selkirkshire, ready for his return. He had wild ideas of holding a New Year's Eve party there to welcome in 1970 – although, knowing Chay as I do, I would not have been surprised if he had lost interest in it by the time he got back home. As things turned out, there was a considerable delay on the lease, and I could not start decorating until that was through and various repairs had been done. In the end, however, I had lots of people roped in to help : and then I received that fateful telegram : 'Going into Port Elizabeth. Discontinuing voyage. Will you fly out? If answer yes, await further instructions. Commonsense must prevail. Metrobeale.'

When Chay sent that telegram, his intention was that I should sail back with him, although he had not said so. But after he had sent it, he wondered if I would bring Samantha out with me, because if I did I would have to fly back. I replied 'Yes', which did not really help matters, because he had forgotten by that time exactly what he had asked me. Then I received a second telegram, querying my reply, and I sent off another with a bit more explanation. Even so, he did not really know what was going to happen until after I had arrived. Poor soul! I suppose it was all a bit difficult for him after being on his own for three months!

As things turned out, I did not know what the end of my flight would produce, either. Chay's final telegram said that Chick would meet me at Johannesburg airport, and I assumed that Chick would then drive me to Port Elizabeth, pop me on the boat, and wave us both goodbye. When I boarded the aircraft on September 23, I had no idea that I was going to South Africa for a holiday, and my baggage included only two dresses.

And when I stepped off the aircraft and was met not only by Chick and Lisa but by Chay, I could not believe my eyes. Somehow or other, with no passport and only the clothes he stood up in – and even they were not his own – he had come up from Port Elizabeth. It was a wonderful moment, but I was shocked when I saw how thin he had gone. The clothes which I had taken out with me for him, and on which I had paid ten pounds excess baggage charge, would not even fit him. You could have got two Chays into his trousers.

The lathlike Chay of Johannesburg was certainly a far cry from the comfortably rounded character who was now shouting to me as we put a second reef in the mainsail : 'I won't take a sight for a couple of days. Let's see who can make the closest guess to our position on Sunday.' So we guessed – and I guessed best. He could hardly believe it. But there we were on Sunday, December 8 : 19° 1' North, 31° West – and Maureen the winner by miles! I had my weekly all-over wash, which I always looked forward to because it was the only time I treated myself to perfume, and Chay had his Sunday shave – which I looked forward to almost as much because although I had approved of his beard in the early stages I had now decided that it seemed to make him look dirty.

The wind now began to blow about force seven from the east, which was just what we wanted, with a thousand miles still between us and the Azores. We began heading due north, with the idea of edging north-east when we reached the 30° North mark. I started to have the feeling we were going to make it. I wrote in my log: 'Please God, we will. I am counting the days until I have Samantha in my arms. Soon I will be counting the hours.'

We talked endlessly about the Andes, both of us speculating pointlessly on whether there would be any word from Chick awaiting our arrival home to say that the thing was either off or decidedly on. I knew what I hoped, but I kept my hopes to myself.

Still the seas kept coming at us. As the bow sliced them, they broke and swept up and over us and finally dived off the stern, leaving the deck swimming with water and pieces of silvery blue fish scales sticking to the aft compartment door and decorating the cockpit. With the boat kicking and rolling as if it were alive, I felt as if I were permanently on a cakewalk. Every time I tried to walk across the saloon, I was liable to be thrown in any direction but the one I wanted. Carrying a cup of coffee in these conditions was an art I never mastered. I could not help feeling that there was something to be said for an armchair which was comfortable and motionless, on a floor which was civilized enough to remain horizontal. But at least we were galloping along – a hundred and fifteen miles on two consecutive days could not be grumbled at. Chay tried to improve things by staying by the tiller and riding out the squalls with the mainsail and number one still up. We keeled over at an alarming angle while the wind howled its fury at our presumption and the seas attacked us with foam-flecked jaws. It did not take Chay long to decide that discretion had a lot to be said for it. After that, we reduced sail and resigned ourselves to facing the angry elements with *Dytiscus* properly dressed to cope with them. By December 12, we were six hundred and fifty miles short of the Azores and our hopes were balanced on the knife-edge of Nature's whim : we thought we could just about do it if the gods stayed with us, but on the other hand it needed only a couple of days of adverse winds or calms to flatten our chances once and for all.

This, however, was a day which cried out for hopes to stay alive; a day of clear blue sky with just the odd cottonwool cloud crossing over it, and *Dytiscus* skipping along with the help of a steady force five wind. We were encouraged to discuss what we were going to buy everybody for Christmas, and I wrote out our list on the stiff inside cover at the back of my log. Having roughed it out in pencil, I started again and did it rather more neatly in ink, on the last page but one. Then the sound of carols on the radio brought me up with a jerk: it would be too awful if we were not back home before the time for carol-singing had passed. Chay knew just how I was feeling.

'Don't upset yourself, Maureen. We're not beaten yet.'

He poured a glass of whisky each. 'Here's to us.'

I raised the glass he had handed me, and smiled ruefully.

'And Samantha', I said.

14

Backwards to Christmas

Chay Blyth : December 13 – December 25

FRIDAY the Thirteenth did not do much for us. We spent most of the day becalmed, and it was only by coveting every scrap of breeze it offered that we were able to sneak any nearer the Azores. Christmas came inevitably into our conversation. Maureen started it as she poured out our morning cups of coffee.

'All the lights will be on in Regent Street, and everyone will be chasing after their Christmas shopping', she said.

I nodded. 'Santa Claus will be doing a great trade with the children.'

Perhaps I should not have said that. Maureen's reply came as if by reflex action. 'I wonder if Mummy has taken Samantha to see him . . . .'

She was silent for a moment or two, looking out of the saloon window at the inconsequential flotsam which was bobbing by – odd pieces of seaweed, and a football loaded with barnacles. She was suddenly a sad little figure in the sweater and slacks with which she had acknowledged the distinct drop in temperature that had caused her to banish her equatorial shorts. Then, turning towards me again, with a curious, puzzled expression on her face, she startled me by saying : 'You know, we might just as well be dead, mightn't we? The world is going on perfectly well without us. It isn't missing us a bit.'

I was amazed – because this very thought had occurred to me from time to time, both on the present trip and in *English Rose*. It was a thought whose accuracy was unassailable : choose to disappear from the mainstream of humanity, and you might indeed just as well be dead. The world you leave behind does not miss you. As likely as not, it does not even know you have gone. There is no point in wondering, as John and I had wondered, whether it will matter if you pop aboard a ship as a break from rowing your little boat in the middle of nowhere – because the answer is as unmistakable as a palm tree in a pantry. It just will not matter a damn. As far as twentieth century man is concerned, commuting between his nine-to-five desk and his suburban semi-detached, you are as relevant as last week's rice pudding, as dead as the dodo. These are disconcerting thoughts when you are alone on an impassive sea. You have a sense of having stepped out of your grave, to become an invisible observer of the urgent world you have left behind.

You have been away for months, but the world news on your radio never says that anybody has noticed you are not there. It talks – as ours had done the other day – about price increases for cigarettes and alcohol, or air crashes, or international politics, or strikes, or student sit-ins; about all the things it was talking about when you were in the land of the living; But never about you and your shattering decision to disappear from the face of the earth. Your absence has had had all the impact of a sparrow feather hurled at the Great Wall of China by an undernourished three-year-old with rheumatism in both shoulders. You feel you could not have achieved less significance if you had taken a correspondence course in how to do it.

But until Mauren spoke, I had assumed that such thoughts were just another manifestation of Blyth the oddball. Her words opened up the possibility that solitude's effects included a broad band of reactions which were common to everyone who experienced it, instead of being largely different for each person. Survival had suddenly attained a universality of which I had never suspected it. So we began to talk survival, and as survival is a subject which can pin me by the ears at any time we went on talking survival for quite a long time.

We had plenty of time for talking, these frustrating days. Plenty of subjects, too. Our lack of progress for one; our radio for another. Try as we might, we could not contact the Azores to send a cable home, although the Azores were only about six hundred miles away. Yet we could hear New Orleans coastguard, three thousand miles distant, and Boston coastguard, and Casablanca, which were for all practical purposes on the other side of the world.

It was all a bit surprising – but not nearly as surprising as the behaviour of the ship which came our way on the morning of Monday, December 16, when we were still in the grip of the calms and still trying in vain to get through to Azores Radio. It was

Maureen who spotted it when it was on the horizon – it always seemed to be Number One who led the way on ship-spotting – and who caused me to scramble for the binoculars, hoist the ensign and switch on the radio telephone. If we could not raise the Azores, surely we would be able to get some response from a ship which was by comparison within spitting distance. Our hopes rose as we saw it alter course and head downwind, straight towards us. As an extra insurance, I made an R/T flag, by drawing dark blue letters on a white polythene rations bag with a felt-tip pen, and we held it up against the sail to show that we would like to make contact by radio.

Closer and closer came the ship – our post office in the ocean, our link with the life we had opted out of. She came so close that I did not even bother to hoist the M.I.K. flags, which we had got ready in our first heady panic. I dashed below and called her. Nothing. Again I tried. More nothing. I could not believe it. I rejoined Maureen on deck and we stood side by side, all dismay and disbelief, as the ship, from Stockholm, steamed unheeding past, just a hundred yards away on our starboard side. Neither of us spoke : there seemed nothing to say – except, perhaps, to wonder if we really *were* dead after all – as hope altered course again and disappeared over the horizon. It was quite, quite incredible.

Our noon sight told us we had somehow managed to reap enough wind to cover a hundred miles and put us at 30° 20′ North, 34° West. Maureen did no try to hide her feelings. 'If only we could get a decent blow, we could easily make it', she said. 'It's too stupid for words.'

In a bid to fill our sense of emptiness, we even risked our remaining bucket in a speculative fishing exercise. We caught some seaweed which was full of little crabs and seahorses, and that was the end of that operation : they gave Maureen the shudders. During the afternoon, we talked some more about the Andes, with Maureen making some dubious references to the table manners of piranha; and about the 1972 single-handed transatlantic race, with me expressing no reservations at all about Maureen's ability to tackle it successfully. In the evening, we settled to playing cards, with the radio on in the background in case a ship came close enough for us to start again where we had left off after the morning pantomime. The trouble was, ships tended to assume that a yacht did not carry a radio telephone and they did not tune in to the 2182 kc wavelength. Nevertheless, we still could not quite believe that the ship incident had happened : it seemed too unrelated to all things logical – first, that the ship should have changed course to come right up to us, and then that having arrived it should have ignored us. But at least it had confirmed our suspicions that now we had left the world to struggle on without us, the world was content to do just that. We could therefore give our undivided attention to a session of rummy, with the loser committed to making the coffee.

It was at 1945 hours that our concentration came to grief. Over the radio came the word which is guaranteed to galvanize its hearers the world over.

'*Mayday! Mayday! Mayday!*'

It was followed by the short silence which indicated that everyone else had gone off the air to leave it clear. I dropped my cards, dived for a pencil, and prepared to note the details.

'*Mayday! Mayday! Mayday!* This is Sierra Whisky Lima X-ray. This is Sierra Whisky Lima X-ray. This is Sierra Whisky Lima X-ray. *Mayday! Mayday! Mayday!*'

For the next ten minutes, the air was filled with sounds of would-be saviours seeking details of the position and plight of the man behind the voice. The only reply they got, repeatedly, was '*Mayday!*' and his call-sign, of which we could not be certain through the crackling static.

Maureen stared as if she were transfixed at our radio, which had suddenly become the impassive wrapping of one man's crisis.

'The poor soul is absolutely distracted', she said. 'He just won't tell anybody where he is ! He must have a thousand things to do.'

The voices of the frustrated circle of hovering assistance went on pressing for something that would enable them to help. '*What is your position, please, Sierra Whisky Lima X-ray? What is your position, please?*' They came in half a dozen languages, but with one intention. '*Please give your position!*'

'Chay, this is awful ! Doesn't it make you feel useless !'

'*Mayday! Mayday! Mayday!*'

Then, out of the confusion, we heard – as far as we could make out through the crackle and in French accents – that his port side was on fire. Ocean Station Echo and – I think – Bordeaux Radio, plus a covey of ships, went on trying to obtain enlightenment. As far as we could ascertain, one ship seemed able to talk to the man, but it was virtually impossible to prise anything intelligible from the babble and it still appeared that nobody had obtained a position. Then we heard '19 degrees North', and the news that the crew were in lifeboats about a hundred yards away from the ship, where the captain was alone. There was nothing we could do towards hauling anybody aboard from where we were, about eight hundred miles away, so we went on listening in a sort of cold horror. We could picture the darkness of one man's world, somewhere on our own ocean, being lit by tongues of leaping flames, while members of the crew sat forlornly in their small boats, caught up in the swell of an unsympatheic sea, and watched the agony of the ship that had been their home until an hour or two earlier. For us, the reassuring part was the realization of just how many people were intent on helping if they possibly could; the realization that if anything happened to us, there *were* people after all who would care and who – thanks to John Deacon's radio telephone – might be in a position to do something about it. Even at sea, despite our earlier forebodings, it seemed you were not dead until you *were* dead.

We listened for perhaps a couple of hours, hoping in vain for an indication that all was well. I sat on my bunk to write my log : 'We will pray for the master and his crew tonight. Once again, the reminder that on the sea you must never relax. Your guard must be up at all times.'

Next day, we were back from the curious unreality of our role as listeners-in to a real-life drama – back to the reality of our race against the calendar; a race whose prize was Christmas with Samantha; a race whose prize we could see beginning to slip inexorably away from us. We were seven degrees from our goal – about five hundred miles, allowing for the easting – but still we had no wind to help us towards it, and still we had made no contact with the Azores to let Maureen's mother know that in spite of everything we were still safe. Maureen was – as usual – marvellous. She did not complain, although it would have been the most natural thing in the world if she had done. She had agreed to sail from South Africa with me on the understanding that we would be home by Christmas. And now here we were, with *Dytiscus* bobbing purposelessly, the rigging creaking, the stores edging gently against each other, and the disinterested sea making tired rivulets among the barnacle mountains which had formed on our port side as a result of its prolonged submersion during our run with the north-

east winds. How we could do with those winds now! Yet there
was not a whisper; not a hope. We had covered about six thousand
miles from Port Elizabeth, but what did six thousand miles matter,
now that we had a record of seventy miles in three days against us?
We still had a lot of sailing to do, and in seven days' time it would
be Christmas Eve. We saw another ship on the horizon. This time,
hoping to avoid a repetition of the *San Benito* episode, I did not
hesitate about raising the M.I.K. But we received no acknowledgment, and again we watched the horizon swallow a ship which
would have meant so much to our peace of mind if it had taken
the cable that we still had to send home. The following day, it
happened again. And still *Dytiscus* bobbed.

By this time, I was as edgy as a cat at a strange dustbin: as
prickly as a hedghog's housewarming. When everything is nothingness, trivia take on an unaccustomed consequentiality. The inactivity
which had been forced upon us for a week was making me
explosively unpredictable. I looked at the unhelpful heavens and I
offered imprecations without stint. I really put my heart into it.
Any passing sergeant major would have been happy to acknowledge
my proficiency.

Then I remembered what I had said a day or two earlier: *at least
if you're rowing a boat, you can row.* Hell, why not?

'Number One', I yelled, 'we're back in business!'

Maureen, who had been pondering her Christmas presents list,
poked her head out of the saloon in response to the bellow with
which I indicated that inspiration had arrived on deck. Before she
could speak, I trotted out the explanatory footnote.

'We're going to make this blasted boat move if it kills us!
You can be Oxford and I'll be Cambridge.'

'Have an oar', I added, helpfully, offering her a spinnaker boom
which transparently took her by surprise.

'You must be joking!' Maureen might not at that point have
been open to confusion with a nautical almanack, but she did reckon
to know an oar when she saw one. And the boom which I had
removed from where it had been clipped on to the deck had no
pretensions to having anything to do with Putney-to-Mortlake.

'No, I'm not. Look: you take this and I'll have the other one,
and we'll turn them into something to row with.'

'Row? What do you mean? How?'

'All we need are a couple of window-blanking boards lashed on the ends – and bingo! Here come the Vikings!'

'Chay, you're pulling my leg . . . but let's give it a try.'

So we did. We stood side by side, just forward of the mast and on either side of it, dipped our blanking boards into an Atlantic Ocean which took the intrusion without a blink, and heaved on our 'oars' while stainless steel stanchions did duty as rowlocks.

'This is ridiculous!' Maureen was laughing like a studio audience which likes to make sure that the man who is holding up the Applaud sign realizes it can read. Tears were streaming down her face at the sheer absurdity of the enterprise on which we had embarked.

'Ridiculous nothing: this is a serious business . . . .'

I broke off to observe a moment's silence as I caught an almighty crab. Then:

'Good God, woman: don't you know I *always* row the Atlantic?'

Sploosh . . . heave . . . puff. Sploosh . . . heave . . . puff. Sploosh . . . heave . . . puff.

After a minute or two, we fell into something approaching a rowing rhythm. Nothing to be compared with *English Rose* standards, perhaps, but commendable in the context of a thirty-foot yacht.

'I'll have to speak to Mr Nierop about this', I panted. 'Fancy forgetting to fit any rowlocks . . . .'

Sploosh . . . heave . . . puff. I broke into song.

'*I'm rowing backwards for Christmas . . . .*'

Maureen joined in.

'*. . . Across the – phew! – Irish Sea . . . .*'

'*I'm rowing backwards for Christmas. . . .*'

'*It's the only thing for me-eee . . . .*'

It was a performance which would have qualified us for a padded cell unquestioned, if it had been observed by anybody with an eye for these things. But it cheered us both up – and it must have put us every inch of a hundred yards nearer home; a hundred yards nearer that cup of tea made with water fresh from a tap, which was one of the lesser targets that Maureen had fixed her sights on.

The slight breezes we were getting during these empty days were not strong enough for the boat to make sufficient speed for the self-steering gear to have much effect. Six months at sea had stiffened it, and waving an oil can at it did not effect any improvement. So whenever we detected the faintest chance of making some progress we latched on to the tiller and steered by hand. But within half an hour the breeze had gone in any case, and it would keep us waiting another two hours before it whispered from another direction, just strongly enough to overcome the barnacle anchor and edge us ponderously forward. Night after night, after Maureen had gone to bed, I sat up into the small hours, waiting for a sign that progress was again a possibility. I was propped up in my bunk, having a gentle read, at 0215 hours on Thursday, December 19, when there was a bumping, scraping sound on the hull, reminiscent of the day we met the dolphins. I leaped up as if somebody had prodded me with a well-judged bradawl, and I dashed outside. There, I waited for a minute while my eyes adjusted to the darkness – and then, just a yard or two from the boat, saw a tell-tale fin. I flashed my torch, revealing a nine-foot shark – an ugly brute who was obviously unimpressed at finding himself spotlighted. He just lolled around for perhaps two minutes, magnificently contemptuous. Then he slid towards the boat, with all the ease and grace in the world, before dipping smoothly beneath the stern. That was the last I saw of him.

But he had left his calling card, as I discovered when we got up to see what the new day was offering. A suggestion of a breeze tempted us into raising the ghoster and booming out the genoa; but the moment I set the self-steering gear, *Dytiscus* made it quite clear that she was not having any. She began to ziz-zag like a Glaswegian who has been celebrating the latest Rangers-Celtic encounter. I peered over the stern and found that a shark had broken the wire. I fitted a new one after disconnecting the tiller lines and quadrant and pulling the self-steering gear forward while Maureen took the tiller. Then, with the vane again putting up a stout resistance to the wind, we stayed with the tiller for another two hours. We watched a plane pass overhead, a silver glint heading for South America. It would be there in a couple of hours.

Friday, December 20, the day we had hoped to reach the Azores, found us still a good four hundred miles south-west of them. And that was the day the winds came. It was almost as if we were on the conscience of the clerk of the weather. All day, from 1000 hours onwards, we were being whisked north by a force four from the south-west, fairly eating up the miles to Samantha. By evening, we were feeling as if we had achieved something – but by evening, it was apparent that more was to come. The whole horizon was a scowl of clouds, black and brooding, and obviously considering what should be done about us. We were skipping ahead with the ghoster and genoa both boomed out, which is hardly the situation to be caught in by a squall. But every mile we could make was another Samantha mile, and like all sailors in a hurry I decided to wait until the last moment before reducing sail. The result was a near-disaster.

We were hit as if by an invisible hand, with a gusting, howling, blasting battery of blows. And with the squall came the rain : rain in a torrential sheet that lashed us like rain that was really giving its mind to the job. Before we knew it, we were going far faster than was healthy. We scrambled into our sailing suits, then I picked my way forward, steadying myself at every step against the crazed-caterpillar action which *Dytiscus* had adopted the moment the elements gave her the cue. I had to get the sails down faster than I had ever lowered them before. While Maureen was busy in the cockpit, putting a warp over the stern to try to steady the boat, I took a quick look at the speedometer : it was registering fourteen knots – which familiarity with the ways of my speedometer prompted me to judge meant about ten knots, but that was still much too brisk for my peace of mind. The boat was surfing! From my position up front, I was well placed to see the way we were skimming headlong to potential disaster, with the wind right behind us and gathering force by the minute. The stage was set for us to broach – and if the stern were picked up the way it had been picked up when I was in the roaring forties, Maureen would almost certainly be thrown overboard as *Dytiscus* was slammed on her side at ninety degrees to the waves. Neither of us had put on a lifeline in our haste. Fortunately, Maureen was too occupied with her own duties to realize what was happening. Even more fortunately – I was tempted at the time to think of it as a miracle – *Dytiscus* kept before the wind long enough for us to juggle with the sails and lessen the probability of catastrophe. We finished up by running with two reefs in the mainsail, and the storm jib, plus the warp, while the squalls kept hitting us with varying degrees of dedication up to storm force, and a black, black night began to envelop us.

When we went to bed, *Dytiscus* was cutting through the darkness like a small, red knife, while a raging hell buffetted her on all sides. At 0230 hours, hell declared a dividend – a bonus of grumbling thunder and sheet lightning, directly overhead, and hailstones which hammered on the saloon roof as if someone was dragging a huge tin sheet across it. It was like Blackpool Illuminations under siege. We slid six inches deeper into our sleeping bags and prayed for the dawn.

When dawn came, our winds and their attendant excesses had departed, leaving us bobbing along at something like half-a-knot. It was time to face facts. 'Maureen', I said 'we're not going to make it. We're at 34 North and the Azores are 37 degrees 40. That's another two hundred and thirty miles, and the way things look, we're going to be lucky to knock off seventy of them today.'

She took it wonderfully, although I knew what it meant to her. It would be the first Christmas that Samantha would have as a 'person', rather than as a five-month-old bundle of chuckles, and we would not be there to see it. She shrugged, a little philosophical shrug that concealed what she must have been feeling.

'Well, that's it, isn't it? We can't do anything about it. Perhaps we can still be at the Azores by Boxing Day.'

That was a pretty forlorn hope, too, and she knew it – but it was typical of Maureen that she should have uttered it, rather than give way to the frustrations just below the surface.

She was not helped by our continued failure to contact the Azores with our radio. We were beginning to wonder if our transmitter was working, but I did not have much idea how to find out so we felt more or less obliged to accept the situation. In the meantime, we still did not know if our efforts with the M.I.K. flags had resulted in Lloyds' passing on news of our whereabouts to Maureen's mother. We were continuing to have our intermittent encounters with shipping. The ships raised our hopes and we raised our flags, but we never knew whether our performance with the bunting had achieved anything towards getting our position reported. When one tanker came towards us, we hoisted the M.I.K., and the ensign, held up our home-made R/T flag, and called him on the 2182 wavelength during the silence period. The silence period consists of the first three minutes of every quarter of an hour, starting on the hour, and everyone is supposed to keep off the air so that if you have to come up with an emergency call you can feel confident that someone will hear. But our confidence soon disappeared: the tanker passed within two hundred yards and just kept going.

Now that we knew we were going to have our Christmas dinner at sea, we began discussing the menu which Maureen had provided in the Christmas parcel. And then, three days before Christmas, another gale hit us. Life became a thing of bumps and bruises as *Dytiscus* shuddered under the assault of top-heavy walls of grey-green water which crashed cataclysmally across her deck. Maureen was saturated by one foaming cascade as she was sheeting-in. Being Maureen, she saw the funny side of it – which was just as well, because I was uncorking great gusts of laughter from my vantage point on the coach roof.

All day, the sea and the wind put on a terrifying double act which seemed if anything to mount in its intensity as time passed. The self-steering gear kept jumping out of place, and at about midnight I had to do my fourth emergency repair to a broken wire. It was the same the next day, with a force nine wind screaming crazily in the rigging as great blocks of spume-licked sea burst against the yacht. One moment, *Dytiscus* had her nose to the sky; the next, she was plummetting downwards, bunkered in hell's own golf course and waiting for Nature to play the next stroke.

That morning, December 23, brought us the best Christmas present we could have wished for : a ship, ploughing towards us with the waves crashing over her bows. The thrill was the realization that here at last was a ship which was interested in us. She circled us five times, then came in closer, downwind of us : obviously, the master of *Meta Reith* knew all about the difficulties caused to sailing boats by bigger craft which hog the wind. We did some more spadework with the M.I.K. and the R/T sign, whereupon the ship flagged, 'Keep clear, I am manoeuvring with difficulty.' That rather interested me, because there was nothing I could do to keep clear. Then he followed up with, 'I have a doctor on board.' After this, *Meta Reith*'s radio operator came on the air to ask if we needed help. Apparently, it was a German ship of about a thousand tons, which was bound for New York but was considering going to Bermuda because of a possible dock strike at New York. The help we needed, I told him, was an exact position, as I had not been able to take a sight for three days, and a telegram relay service.

He obliged most readily, and I found I was only seventeen miles out of my dead reckoning – not bad, considering I was under self-steering gear and trailing no log. He also accepted the cable which we hoped would allay the anxiety which we were sure must have

been building up in Newcastle: 'Calms. All well. Position 36° 11'
North, 29° 25' West Flying Azores. E.T.A. 29th. Merry Christmas.
Reply. M.C.'

He traded us some alarming news in exchange for our telegram:
a severe storm was expected in our area the following day.

We talked a litlle longer, then we wished each other a happy
Christmas. It was time for *Meta Reith* to go. Number One and I
stood together on deck as the smart, black-hulled ship turned and
headed away. Now that we knew our telegram was on its way,
Christmas was not going to be as bad as it might have been after all
– assuming, of course, that tomorrow's storm was not going to upset
the applecart altogether. Certainly, Maureen's mother would have a
load taken from her mind when she received our message later in
the day.

Our priority now was to prepare for the fury yet to come. We
reduced sail to storm jib only, lashed down everything on deck
that it was possible to lash down, and we put food, flares, water and
a knife ready below, in case we had to take to the life raft. Not
that I expected this to happen: *Dytiscus,* I was sure, could take
whatever was coming. Maureen really put her back into the preparations, although she readily admitted that she was sure she would
have been happier to have had the storm take us by surpirse.

'I have pains in my neck and all across the shoulders – and I'm
sure it's only tension', she said. 'It's all right for you, staying all
calm and collected. I probably wouldn't be worried, either, if I'd
been in hurricanes in a rowing boat or into the roaring forties.'

'Yes', I said, 'but look at it this way: what on earth would we
do if we were *both* crackers?'

Christmas Eve brought our sixth wedding anniversary and found
us lying a-hull two hundred miles from the Azores in a force ten
storm which had leaped at us in the night and hurled the pair of
us across the saloon as the yacht keeled crazily over on one side.
I went on deck and took down the storm jib while Maureen, who
had waved me upstairs with a home-made anniversary card, set
about getting the breakfast ready. Towards mid-morning, things
seemed to go considerably calmer, but after about an hour battle
was joined again with even greater ferocity. From the top of a
wave, we could look down into an eddying valley thirty feet below;
in the valley, we held our breath as we watched to see what the next
wave would do. Each wave was a mountain – an old mountain,

wrinkled by the wind and greyed by the foam which scuttered about its rolling peak. Time after time, our view from the saloon was blurred as several hundreweights of water pounded the roof and washed down the windows. Maureen could not understand why the windows did not break. I could not understand, either, but omitted to say so : I thought Maureen had enough to worry about without confessions like that from me, so I just went on marvelling silently at what was another manifestation of Ronald Nierop's insistence on building for strength. One wave did burst through the air vent, soaking both beds and sleeping bags. It was an alarming moment, but at least it helped to take Maureen's mind off what was going on outside while she organized a dry-the-same-day service with our only hot water bottle.

That night, we had hoped to go to midnight Mass and to put Samantha's presents round the tree on our return home. But thanks largely to the relief of having got our telegram off and to the realization that we were not really all that far from home, we could harbour thoughts like that one without hurt. We had already decided that whatever sort of Christmas Samantha had next day, she would have another one when we were with her again.

For us, Christmas morning was a morning of continuing storm, with only the storm jib set and *Dytiscus* continuing to stand up – when she was not lying down – to her savaging. While we did our best to cope with our switchback surroundings, the wireless fed us an uninterrupted diet of carols and Christmas talks. Christmas dinner, on our laps in the absence of the table, was a meal which we are unlikely to forget, either for its content or its circumstances. Soup, then pheasant with potatoes, peas and carrots, followed by Christmas pudding. The whole lot came out of the special pack which Maureen had prepared, and it was magnificent. The only drawback was that we had to pour condensed milk, instead of brandy, over the pudding. We washed the whole lot down with whisky, then we listened to the Queen's Christmas message and heard the news that the Apollo astronauts were on their way back from their moon trip. I blinked mock despair across the saloon.

'Those lads are going to beat us home, even after giving us a couple of months' start.'

But the situation did not seem too bad, somehow. We had exchanged Christmas cards – I had done my best with a do-it-yourself one, from me and Samantha, and Maureen had given me the one she had packed in Portsmouth – and Maureen had surprised me with a stocking full of nuts, spangles, Smarties, chewing gum, After Eights, razor blades, after-shave, and other goodies.

When I saw that lot, I realized what a tribute they were to the stretching qualities of Jack Gregory's nylon socks. Jack is a member of the Royal Southern Yacht Club with a sock factory in Mansfield, Nottinghamshire, and he had wanted me to bring three hundred pairs of socks with me before I began my trip. Do not waste time washing them, he said: throw them away. But that had struck me as being a bit extravagant, and liable to lead to sock-choked oceans, so in the end we compromised at fifty pairs.

The Christmas parcel also contained my present – a silk Paisley-pattern cravat. I had a problem, in that I was not equipped for giving Christmas presents, but I overcame that in one masterstroke: I gave Maureen an IOU for a dress and a pair of shoes. Maureen entered into the game at once: she gave it me back in exchange for a cameo brooch IOU.

And now, chock full of dinner, we both felt cosy and bloated and happy. Christmas is Christmas, even when the Atlantic is having apoplexy on the other side of a couple of thicknesses of fibreglass. Especially when you are sharing it with the girl who has backed you all the way in a crazy undertaking for the second time in two years. Especially whene there is a little citizen called Samantha due back in the family circle any day now.

I raised my glass and grinned contentment at my crew.

'Here's to the mad Blyths', I said.

15

A Note at the End

Maureen Blyth

I T took us longer than we expected to reach the Azores, because the weather died on us after it had carried us well off our course. The result was that we did not put into Ponta Delagada until the morning of Sunday, December 29. It poured with rain all day, but we had a look round and exchanged notes with one or two sailing people we met, before returning to our mooring to spend the night on the boat. I would not have slept so soundly if I had known what we were to learn the following day: that it would cost us a thousand pounds to ship *Dytiscus* home.

That, however, was the situation with which we were confronted when we enquired at the offices of the shipping authorities. The counter clerk was sympathetic but regretful: if we did not want to find a thousand pounds, we would either have to sail *Dytiscus* home or abandon her.

I was appalled. Throughout the dreadful calms and the terrifying seas which had been a feature of my first experience of sailing, I had been buoyed up by the thought that once we reached the Azores we were as good as home. It was not that I was not enjoying my voyage: simply that I was missing Samantha more with every passing day, and longing for the moment when I could take her into my arms again. *Samantha, it's Mummy. Mummy home again – and look who I've brought with me!* What a moment that would be! Several times on the trip, a lump had come to my throat at the very thought of it. And now that we had arrived at the place we had been thinking of as home, we were being told that we had another three weeks' sailing in front of us, through the North Atlantic in winter, with all the frightening possibilities which that entailed, in a boat which had already had more than six months of the sort of punishment for which it had never been intended.

I began to feel that the whole venture had been fated from the day that Chay had sailed off down the Hamble. First, the speedometer had broken, then the water had got into the petrol and there had been the rudder trouble; then the servo blades had broken in quick succession; then we had been dogged by all those calms when we had been trying to race for home. And now, this.

I knew what Chay was going to say before he said it. I could see what it was costing him to say it, because he knew what the words would do to me.

'There's nothing for it, Maureen. I'm afraid we've just got to sail her home.'

We cabled Mummy to tell her of the change of plan. Then at dawn on Sunday, January 5, after we had given ourselves a week's rest, we sailed — towed out of harbour by a pilot boat because there was not a breath of wind to be had, but assured by the pilot that there would be a bit outside.

This turned out to be as impressive an understatement as we had encountered for some time. At 8.30 a.m., we had our ghosting genoa and mainsail up, but by 12.15 p.m. we were down to storm jib and two reefs in the mainsail, with a force eight gale driving short, sharp waves into us like so many green cannon-shot, and visibility down to half a mile. Every wave produced a surprising, whip-like noise on the hull, and the rigging joined in as the wind screamed through it. Most of the day, I huddled into my sleeping bag and tried to think clearly of what I would have to do if we had to take to the life raft. By the evening, the gale had become a storm, and *Dytiscus* had begun to slew round alarmingly in the face of the battering she was receiving. Conditions were far worse now than they had been when we were coming round the Cape of Storms. Every few minutes, the boat shuddered and twisted round, and she was constantly keeled right over on her starboard side. I was aware of her doing things which she had never done before. It seemed as if she was being stopped dead on the top of a wave, with the bow trying to go in one direction and the stern in another. I tried to imagine how much worse than this it would be to face the storm in the life raft; failed totally to picture what it must have been like for Chay and John— not in a yacht but a rowing boat, not in a storm but a hurricane. And not in one hurricane but two. I thought of the words which Chay had brought home with *English Rose*. *Patience. Above all, patience.*

To make it worse, we were not even going the way we wanted

to go : we had had to turn about and head south, because Chay had said that to go on into the storm was a sheer impossibility. With every minute, we were going further from home.

It was 6.45 p.m., and I was dreading the long night that was to come. I was chilled to the bone already, and the only thing I could be certain of was that I would be colder still in the small hours. I cupped my hands over my mouth and breathed into them, hoping that this would do something to warm my face – and warm my hands, too, because they were like lumps of ice. Again and again, blockbusting barrages of water thumped the saloon while *Dytiscus* pitched and swayed like something crazed. It was almost as if she were in her last agony. *Dear God, please bring us home.*

Chay had been up on deck. Now he came below, and it seemed as if the sight of me curling up small, all pale and interesting, startled him. He looked down at me for a long moment, and I could see that something or other was whirling around in his mind. Then he spoke, urgently and finally.

'We're going back to the Azores. The storm's getting worse and I've no right to ask you to risk it.'

His words made me want to cry with relief. I did cry. It was as if they had whisked a cold hand from round my heart. Commonsense had prevailed, as it had prevailed when Chay had realized the foolhardiness of going on when the boat had kept broaching after he had left East London. We could leave *Dytiscus* at the Azores, fly home, and return in the summer for what ought to be a wonderful sail back to Portsmouth. Our obligation was to Samantha, and that obligation was that we should not do anything stupid.

We altered course, while cavernous jaws waited to swallow us and foam dripped saliva off the coach roof to mark where their last attempt at a meal had failed to achieve fulfilment. Water kept finding its way inside the boat. In twenty-four hours, we baled out eight gallons, and that still left us with a couple of inches all over the saloon floor. Both sleeping bags and all our clothes were soaked, and the storm, as if sensing that its chances of doing something disastrous were slipping away, built up to force eleven, gusting twelve. That means occasional winds of at least sixty-four knots.

It went on all through the night and all the following day. Then, incredibly, on Tuesday, January 7, when we had returned to within twenty miles of our destination, we sailed into a virtual calm. Whatever our earlier thoughts about calms, this one at least gave

me the chance to get everything dry before the pilot boat came out
to meet us at the Sao Miguel breakwater at 11 p.m.

Our final meal of the voyage was dinner. As dinners go, this
was not a world-beater. I had to mash the frozen chips we had
bought in the Azores because we were short of fat to fry them;
the caviar was imitation and unpleasant; the asparagus was second
quality; the Portuguese wine was too dry. But whoever it was who
said something about the proof of the pudding, he knew what he
was talking about: Chay, indefatigable to the end, ate everything
I gave him.

And this time, too-dry wine and all, it was my turn to suggest
a toast. We chinked glasses.

'To the Blyths again', I said.

* * * * * *

Half a year had gone by since we said goodbye to *Dytiscus*, the
boat which Chay sailed solo for nine thousand miles, which we have
been told is further than anyone else has sailed a glass fibre production nonstop yacht; the boat which gave us memories that we shall
treasure for ever. The three months we had shared on board were
three months of closeness, understanding, patience; three months
which tested the strength of our love, the unity of our purpose.
The voyage together was the opportunity of a lifetime which is
never likely to occur again, and I would not have liked to have
missed a day of it. It showed me that ours is a bond which can survive the strains and frustrations of being alone together, day after
day, week after week, in a little thirty-foot yacht with a saloon
which measures only about ten feet by eight. And more than survive:
grow stronger. The emptiness of the calms and the teamwork of
the storms made us realize in a hundred different ways our impor-
tance to each other; made us aware of what a true marriage partnership can really mean – although if anyone had asked me before I
flew out to South Africa I would have said I thought ours was a
pretty terrific partnership already. The debt we owe to *Dytiscus* is
one we can never hope to repay.

Chay had planned to fly back to the Azores with Chris Waddington and Frank Allen, and they will sail the yacht home together.
I have decided not to go this time, because it is too soon for me
to be able to bear to be parted from Samantha again, and Samantha
is too young to come sailing just yet.

Samantha is the overriding factor to be considered when I make my decision about the 1972 Single-handed Transatlantic Race. I am approaching the race in all seriousness, and I am determined to complete the necessary five hundred miles of solo sailing in one trip which is the basic qualification. I am sure I can overcome my fears of the dark, and I have the opportunity now to learn to do so : I have been offered a boat in which to take part when the time comes. Everything, in other words, is geared for my being there, with Chay and the other competitors, when the starting gun is fired. Apart from anything else, I would love to see the look on Chay's face if he completes the course and finds me waiting to welcome him !

But, in a man's world, while it is all right for a man to go off doing adventurous things, it is not at all the same if a woman considers following suit. She is told that she is leaving her children behind, that she is neglecting her responsibilities, that she is doing this and doing that. Almost certainly, this will happen to me in 1972, if my name appears among the entries – although this is the least of my worries : when people are talking about me, they are giving someone else a rest.

In the final analysis, it all comes back to Samantha. Nothing else really matters. I think this, in the nature of things, is where men and women differ in their outlook. To a woman, a child is her world; to a man, the world merely includes the child, though he may worship that child as he worships nothing else – the way Chay worships Samantha. I shall not know – I cannot know – what my decision will be until much nearer the time when it has to be made.

When the time comes Chay may be racing across the Atlantic himself, climbing the Andes, or perhaps something quite different. New ideas are readily seized upon by this husband of mine if they offer a bigger challenge than the one he is planning. Perhaps it could be round the world again – but the opposite way against the Roaring Forties this time, as no one has done that alone non-stop.

Meanwhile, Chay still talks about the Andes and the Amazon. Everything is costed; everything is down on paper. While we were on the boat, we got down to basic details of equipment, navigational and medical requirements. Nevertheless, I could not help feeling that he was not all that keen on the idea – which pleased me, because I believed he had jumped into it all too quickly. And anyway, it would be nice to have him at home, because he has already missed so much of Samantha's growing up process.

But my doubts about his enthusiasm disappeared as soon as we arrived home and I saw his reaction to finding the place bristling with letters from Chick, who was as keen as mustard, and from Lisa, who was asking where she was going to stay while the lads were away, and if I was going over to stay with her, and where the children would go to school. I thought, 'My God, she's serious!'

If Chay finally commits himself to this, or any other similar plan, I shall not try to stand in his way. I know that for Chay these things are necessary. People who have still not got over the idea that a six-year marriage can withstand an Atlantic row and a bid to sail round the world will undoubtedly ask: 'Whatever will Maureen do this time?'

The answer is not all that complicated. Maureen will do what Maureen did last time and the time before.

Maureen will help.